T0196990

Food of Bodhisattvas

Buddha Shakyamuni

༄༅། །ཁབས་དགར་ཚོགས་དྲུག་རང་གྲོལ་གྱི་
གསུང་འབུམ་ལས་ཕའི་ཉེས་དམིགས་དང་
ལེགས་ལ་ཁད་བདུད་རྩིའི་རྒྱ་རྒྱུན་
བཞུགས།

པཎྜི་ཀུ་རའི་སྐུ་བསྐུར་མ་ཐུན་ཚོགས་ནས་
སྐུ་བསྐུར་ཞུས།།

Food of Bodhisattvas

Buddhist Teachings
on Abstaining from Meat

Shabkar Tsogdruk Rangdrol

Translated by the
Padmakara Translation Group

Shambhala
Boston & London
2004

Shambhala Publications, Inc.
Horticultural Hall
300 Massachusetts Avenue
Boston, Massachusetts 02115
www.shambhala.com

Printed in the United States of America
⊗ This edition is printed on acid-free paper that meets
the American National Standards Institute z39.48 Standard.
♻ Shambhala Publications makes every effort to print on recycled paper.
For more information please visit www.shambhala.com.
Distributed in the United States by Random House, Inc.,
and in Canada by Random House of Canada Ltd

Library of Congress Cataloging-in-Publication Data

Żabs-dkar Tshogs-drug-ṅan-grol, 1781–1851.
[Rmad byuṅ sprul pa'i glegs bam. Sa'i ñes dmigs. English]
Food of Bodhisattvas: Buddhist teachings on abstaining from meat/
Shabkar Tsogdruk Rangdrol; translated by the Padmakara Translation
Group.—1st ed.
p. cm.
In English; translated from Tibetan.
Includes bibliographical references.
ISBN 978-1-59030-116-6 (pbk. : alk. paper)
1. Meat—Religious aspects—Tantric Buddhism. 2. Tantric
Buddhism—China—Tibet—Customs and practices. 3. Żabs-dkar
Tshogs-drug-ṅan-grol, 1781–1851. I. Żabs-dkar Tshogs-drug-ṅan-grol,
1781–1851. Legs bśad bdud rtsi'i chu rgyun. English. II. Padmakara
Translation Group. III. Title.
BQ7610 .Z33 2004
294.3'5693—dc22 2003026682

Contents

Foreword

I am very happy that the Padmakara Translation Group has translated these wonderful texts. Lama Shabkar drew attention to the fact that animals, insects, and even shellfish are sentient beings, and because all of them cherish life and have feelings, they deserve to be respected just as human beings do.

If we Buddhists—especially if we consider ourselves to be on the Mahayana path—wish to live according to the Buddha's teachings, then, as is said again and again in these texts, we must definitely avoid harming any living beings, whether directly or indirectly. This means that we must neither kill nor torture them ourselves, nor induce anyone else to do so.

When we enter upon the path of Dharma, we go for refuge in the Three Jewels, taking the Buddhas and Bodhisattvas as our witnesses. Repeating after the preceptor, we say, "Taking refuge in the Dharma, I vow not to harm any living being." It is difficult to pretend not to know that we have said this, or to think that we can interpret these very clear words in some other way.

And so it is my wish that we may all develop love and compassion for all sentient beings, considering each of them as though they were our own dear children.

The Padmakara Translation Group gratefully acknowledges the generous support of the Tsadra Foundation in sponsoring the translation and preparation of this book.

Translators' Introduction

People who know little about Buddhism but are fairly familiar with its teachings on nonviolence and compassion often assume that Buddhists are vegetarians. It is with surprise and sometimes a touch of disappointment that they discover that many (though by no means all) Buddhists, East and West, do in fact eat meat. Leaving aside the host of factors, private or social, affecting the behavior of individuals, the general attitude of Buddhists toward the consumption of meat has been conditioned by historical and cultural factors, with the result that attitudes vary from country to country. In their traditional setting, for example, the Mahayana Buddhists of China and Vietnam are usually strictly vegetarian. On the other hand, it is not uncommon for Japanese—and almost always the case for Tibetans—to eat meat. And as Buddhism has spread to Europe, America, and elsewhere, it has seemed natural for new disciples to adopt the attitudes and practices typical of the tradition they follow.

Tibet was the one country in Asia to which the entire range of Buddhist teaching was transmitted from India, and Tibetans have, from the eighth century till the present, been deeply committed to the teachings of the Mahayana in both its sutric and tantric forms—studying, reflecting upon, and bringing into living experience its teachings on wisdom and universal compassion. It is well known, moreover, that these teachings and the attitudes they engendered on the popular level exerted a powerful influence on the relationship between the Tibetans and their natural surroundings. European visitors to Tibet and the Himalayan region before the Chinese invasion were often struck by the richness and docility of the wildlife, which had become fearless of human beings in a country where hunting was rare and universally condemned. Yet the fact remains that Tibetans in general have always been, and still are, great meat eaters. This is mainly due to climate and geography, since large portions of the country lie at altitudes where the cultivation of crops is impossible.

Long habit, of course, gives rise to deep-seated predilection and, despite their religious convictions, many Tibetans living in other parts of the world have not changed their diet. This, in itself, is not very surprising. It is difficult for everyone to abandon the habits of a lifetime, and one of the first impulses of travelers and immigrants the world over is to import or procure their own kind of food. In any case, like the rest of humanity, many Tibetans find meat delicious and eat it with relish. But if this was and is the norm, both in Tibet and among Tibetans in exile, the daily practice of the Mahayana— constant meditation on compassion and the Bodhisattva's commitment to liberate all beings from their sufferings— inescapably calls into question the eating of meat. As a rule, Tibetan Buddhists, even confirmed meat eaters, are not insensitive to this. Many freely admit that the consumption of a food indissociable from the intentional killing of animals is less than ideal and is unsuitable for Buddhist practitioners. Many Tibetans make the effort to abstain from meat on holy days and at certain sacred seasons of the year. Many express an admiration for vegetarianism; and it is rare to find Tibetan lamas who do not praise and advocate it for those who are able, even if, for whatever reason, the lamas consume meat themselves.

Among the Tibetans living in exile in India and Nepal, countries where alternative nourishment is available and where the practice of meat eating is culturally less ingrained, a change of custom seems to be slowly taking shape, particularly among the younger generations.[1] A number of monasteries, including Namgyal Dratsang, the monastery of His Holiness the Dalai Lama, no longer allow meat to be cooked in their kitchens; and even if the personal practice of individual monastics is left to their own decision, a small but growing number of monks and nuns have abandoned meat eating altogether.

For Western practitioners, the situation is rather different. Unlike the Tibetans, we live mostly in areas where a wide variety of wholesome vegetable food is easy to obtain. Nevertheless, we belong to a culture in which religious and ethical traditions sanction and encourage the eating of meat. The compassionate attitude toward animal life, which is inherent to the Buddhist outlook and with which, despite their nutritional habits, Tibetans are as a rule profoundly imbued, is lacking in our society. To a large extent, the humane treatment of domestic animals, where it exists in the modern world, is dictated by sentimentality and curtailed by financial considerations; it is not based on the understanding that animals are living beings endowed with minds and feelings, whose predicament in samsara is essentially no different from our own. In any case, for many Westerners who have become Buddhists, who are carnivores both by habit and desire, the challenge on the question of meat eating posed by Buddhism in general and by the Mahayana in particular tends to be dampened by the fact that, for the reasons just explained, Tibetans have rarely been able to give more than theoretical guidance, albeit sincere.

The situation has been further complicated by the perpetuation in the West of a number of "traditional" rationalizations used to condone the eating of meat by Buddhists. These are often adopted—a little too easily and uncritically, perhaps—by Westerners unable or unwilling to consider an alternative lifestyle. They include the concept of threefold purity, the idea that animals gain a connection with the Dharma (and are therefore benefited) when their flesh is eaten by practitioners, and various other notions derived from a distorted reading of the tantras. As Shabkar demonstrates, these arguments are either false or only half true and call for a careful, honest interpretation. The most that can be said for them is that they are very understandable, very human attempts to salve tender consciences, invoked often apologetically and without much conviction when abstention from meat seems too difficult. In ordinary circumstances and where ordinary people are concerned, it is surely a mistake to regard them as expressions of valid principle.

In any case, it is important to be aware that in Tibet there exists and has always existed another point of view. This was present from the earliest days of Buddhism in the country. It was powerfully reaffirmed by the teaching of Atisha and his Kadampa followers and has been upheld by a few heroic individuals in every subsequent generation. As the texts translated in this book will show, Shabkar was one of this glorious company—Bodhisattva practitioners of both the sutras and the tantras, whose love of others and whose awareness of their sufferings was such that they abstained from meat, at the cost of great personal hardship, in a difficult and unyielding environment. In his discussion of the issues involved, Shabkar raises profound questions regarding various aspects of the Buddha Dharma at its Pratimoksha, Mahayana, and Vajrayana levels and, as a compassionate but clear-sighted observer of humanity, throws a fascinating light on the society and religion of his time.

THE AUTHOR

Shabkar Tsogdruk Rangdrol[2] (1781–1851) left behind numerous volumes of writings,[3] two of which comprise a detailed autobiography, one of the most popular and inspiring in Tibetan literature. In it, amid a wealth of poetry and song, he recounts a spiritual career that began with the first stirrings of renunciation in his early childhood and culminated with perfect attainment.[4] He spent almost the whole of his life in retreat or else as a wandering pilgrim, visiting many of the sacred places of Tibet and the Himalayan region—from Amdo and the Mongolian border in the north where he was born, to the great mountain range of Amnye Machen and thence to the central provinces of Ü and Tsang, to the ravines of Tsari, and to Kailash, the sacred mountain in the west, and then south to the valley of Kathmandu in Nepal. He was an utterly free spirit, living on the fringes of society. He spent most of his time in solitude, high in the mountains, attended only, if at all, by those of his closest disciples who were able and willing to share the hardships imposed by the physical environment and savor the perfect freedom that comes from the complete abandonment of worldly concerns. He was untouched by social and ecclesiastical conventions and, though an ordained monk, was never closely associated with any of the great monastic establishments, although he visited and endowed them whenever he could, sometimes with spectacular generosity. Loving the monastic discipline yet immersed in the yogic practice of the Secret Mantra, he must have cut an eccentric figure on his frequent pilgrimages, wearing his patched monastic skirt and the white shawl and long hair of a yogi.

Shabkar's unusual attire was an accurate reflection of his personality and spiritual endeavor. As monk and yogi, he gathered within his practice the Hinayana path of monastic renunciation, the Mahayana path of universal compassion, and the yogic path of the Secret Mantra—the three vehicles of Tibetan Buddhism, implemented according to the gradual scheme so much associated with the Kadampa tradition. Although by Shabkar's time the Kadampas no longer existed as a separate lineage, their teaching on the *Lamrim,* or stages of the path, had exerted a pervasive influence on all four schools of Tibetan Buddhism, inspiring the composition of great and seminal writings that have dominated the religious life of Tibetans until the present day: *The Mind at Rest* of Gyalwa Longchenpa, Je Gampopa's *Jewel Ornament of Liberation*, the Vidyadhara Jigme Lingpa's *Treasury of Precious Qualities*, and of course *The Great Exposition of the Stages of the Path* by Je Tsongkhapa himself. Following Atisha's injunction, Shabkar's outer behavior was marked by the pure discipline of monastic ordination; inwardly, he was a lifelong practitioner and advocate of *lojong*, the mind-training teachings focused on relative and absolute *bodhichitta*; secretly, he was an accomplished yogi who brought to fruition the esoteric teachings of the tantras, especially the highest and most secret instructions of

Dzogchen and Mahamudra. The Hinayana, Mahayana, and Vajrayana were all united in his practice, which he brought to a state of perfect realization.

Shabkar's attitude toward the different schools of Tibetan Buddhism was unclouded by even the slightest trace of sectarian bias. No doubt this was due primarily to his free and independent lifestyle, uncomplicated by institutional allegiances or dependence on benefactors. He lived an entirely hand-to-mouth existence. He had no fixed abode and reduced his own needs to an absolute minimum. The devotion of his disciples often resulted in rich donations, which were speedily dispatched in either religious offerings or gifts of charity. The Dharma was for him a matter of personal insight and training, not of allegiance to a school. He loved the Buddha's teaching in all its manifestations, and his attitude to all traditions was one of unfeigned devotion.

Once, early in life, when visiting the great Gelugpa monastery of Labrang Tashikhyil in Amdo, Shabkar prayed to be able to practice the Dharma perfectly in a manner unstained by prejudice. Referring to this event in his autobiography, he quotes the fifth Panchen Lama declaring the authenticity of all the schools of Tibetan Buddhism, and comments, "In accordance with these words, I always cultivated respectful devotion toward the teachings and teachers, seeing them all as pure."[5] A particularly striking feature of Shabkar's religious personality was the degree to which he combined the teachings of the Nyingmapas with those of the Gelugpas, two schools that are often considered to be poles apart. This must have been favored by the social environment of the region in which he grew up, far from the centers of political power, where practitioners of all traditions lived close to each other and communicated freely.

His own roots were among the Nyingmapa yogis of Rekong in Amdo, famous for the purity of their *samaya* and the
miraculous powers resulting from their spiritual accomplish-
ments. It was here that his religious training began, and it is
evident from his later life that the teaching he received there,
in word and example, left an indelible mark on his character.
At the age of twenty, he received monastic ordination from
the great Gelugpa abbot and scholar Arik Geshe Jampel Gyaltsen Özer, who advised Shabkar to seek out his root guru, the
great Nyingmapa master Chögyal Ngakyi Wangpo. It was from
the latter that Shabkar received all the teachings of the Old
Translation school, up to and including the *trekchö* and *thögal*
instructions of the Great Perfection, which were to form the
core of his personal practice. Nevertheless, as he recounts in
his biography, Shabkar frequently received transmissions and
initiations of the new traditions, among them his beloved
Migtsema, the celebrated prayer to Tsongkhapa as the jewel
ornament of the Land of Snow. Later, on his journeys, he
took delight in visiting the great Gelugpa foundations in the
central provinces of Ü and Tsang, where he made lavish offerings and requested teachings. He also made pilgrimages to the
great monastery of Sakya, where he received empowerments
from the sons of Wangdu Nyingpo, the thirty-third throne
holder.[6] And while in the vicinity, he did not fail to pay his
respects to the monastery of Jonang Ganden Puntsoling, the
former seat of Taranatha Kunga Nyingpo, a copy of whose
teachings he had printed from the wooden blocks still preserved there.[7] Finally, he was completely at home among the
Kagyupa yogis of Mount Kailash and elsewhere. Reading
Shabkar's life, with its atmosphere of serene devotion and
universal respect for all traditions, one would hardly guess the

depth of sectarian animosity that had plagued the social history of Tibet for generations. So powerful and so genuine was
Shabkar's reverence for all the traditions of Tibetan Buddhism
that he has been celebrated as the manifestation of different
personages within these same traditions. He is often venerated as an emanation of Manjushrimitra (*'jam dpal bshes
gnyen*), one of the patriarchs of the Dzogchen lineage of the
Nyingma school. He has been recognized as the incarnation
of the master Ngulchu Gyalse Thogme, much venerated by
the Sakyapas, and as the rebirth of Chengawa Lodrö Gyaltsen,
a close disciple of Je Tsongkhapa. It is, however, as the emanation of Jetsün Milarepa, one of the greatest masters of the
Kagyu school and most beloved figures in the Tibetan tradition, that Shabkar is most celebrated. In terms of lifestyle,
talent, perseverance, and accomplishment, it was surely in the
footsteps of Milarepa that Shabkar most obviously trod.

Shabkar was famous for his affection and concern for animals. His attitude was an expression not only of personal
sympathy and aesthetic appreciation; it was rooted in his understanding of Buddhist teaching. For Shabkar, as for other
Buddhists, animals are to be considered first and foremost as
living beings caught like ourselves in the sufferings of samsara.
However different and strange their physical form, and however rudimentary their intellectual and emotional faculties,
they are nevertheless endowed with mind and are, in the most
basic sense, persons. They cling, no less than humans, to the
notion of self. They therefore long for happiness and fulfillment according to their kind, and they suffer when they fail
to attain it. Compared with humans, animals are of course at
a great disadvantage. Their minds are obscured to a much
greater degree by ignorance, and they are overwhelmed by the

strength of instinct. They may possess sense faculties far more powerful and acute than those of human beings, but their intelligence is not adapted to the reception of the Dharma and the implementation of methods that enable the mind to evolve from a state of bondage into freedom.

In his long years of silent retreat high in the mountains and on his solitary treks through the Tibetan wilderness, Shabkar had no doubt many occasions to watch animals at close range and to observe their ways. Such opportunities, coupled with the extreme simplicity of Shabkar's own life-style, must have further enhanced the natural empathy that he felt toward animals and which we sense on numerous oc-casions in his autobiography. His life in the wild, with little to eat and only meager shelter from the elements, must have brought him an appreciation of the hardships and dangers that are the natural lot of wild animals. He must often have been cold and hungry and must have witnessed the fragility and suffering of animals confronted by the unpredictable changes of climate and the menace of their natural predators. He certainly felt a fellowship with animals, and they too, in the course of his long sojourns in solitary retreat, must have grown accustomed to the innocuous presence of that strange human. Shabkar would occasionally speak to them and some-times—in the chattering of crows, for example, or the plain-tive cries of the cuckoo—he would imagine them speaking to him or to each other. He once gave simple spiritual instruc-tions to a herd of *kyang,* or wild asses, which seemed to stay and listen, and on one occasion he himself received a heartfelt teaching from an old sheep. It is clear from his writings that he was often moved by the beauty of the animals and derived comfort from their companionship. Very often it was the call of birds and the murmuring of insects that prompted him to spiritual insights, which he then recorded in his songs.

From his earliest youth, Shabkar was appalled by the treatment meted out to animals by human beings. In the first pages of his autobiography, he records a childhood experience that was to mark him for the rest of his life.

> One autumn, we had an excellent harvest. Everyone, from all the different households, rich and poor, said that we should celebrate. This of course meant the slaughtering of many scores of sheep. It was a terrible sight. I was horrified and filled with pity. I couldn't bear to be at the slaughtering ground and had to go away and wait till it was all over. When they had finished the killing, I came back and saw the carcasses of the sheep lying on the ground and being cut into pieces. I thought to myself, "These people are doing something terribly wrong, and they are doing it even though they know that they will have to suffer the consequences in their future lives. When I grow up, I will only ever live according to the Dharma. I will completely turn my back on such evil behavior." And I made this promise to myself again and again.
>
> [KWGJ (*The King of Wish-
> Granting Jewels*), f16]

Throughout his life, Shabkar, like any other Buddhist teacher, gave instructions on the law of karma, and he encouraged his listeners to refrain from killing, sometimes with impressive results. Like his older contemporary, Jigme Lingpa, he made it his practice to save the lives of animals by buying them and setting them free. In one of his songs, he records that by the age of fifty-six (he was to live to the age of seventy) he had ransomed the lives of several hundred thousand animals.[8] It was, however, during his early adulthood, on the occasion of a pilgrimage to Lhasa, that an experience occurred that was to prove a turning point in his personal lifestyle. Amid his various visits to shrines and monasteries and the paying of respects to lamas and other religious and political dignitaries, Shabkar had been drawn again and again to the Jokhang, the central temple in the city, which houses the famous Jowo Rinpoche, an image of Shakyamuni Buddha, reputedly made in the latter's own lifetime. This image was and is one of the most revered objects in the Tibetan Buddhist world, and over the centuries it has been the focus of countless offerings and devoted prayers. "One day," Shabkar recalls in his autobiography, "I remained in the presence of the Jowo for a long, long time, and I was praying so intensely that I entered a state of profound absorption. Later, as I was walking along on the outer circumambulation path around the city, I came upon the bodies of many sheep and goats that had been slaughtered. At that moment, the compassion that flooded into me for all the animals in the world that are killed for food was so strong that I could not stand it. I returned to the Jowo Rinpoche, and with prostrations made this vow: 'From today onward, I will abandon the negative act of eating the flesh of beings, each one of whom was once my parent.'" [KWGJ, f201] The year was 1812; Shabkar was thirty-one years old. "From that point onward," he continued, "no one ever killed animals in order to offer me food. I was even told that, when they knew I was about to visit them, my faithful patrons would say, 'This lama does not eat the meat even of animals that have died naturally; we must not leave any meat lying around where he will see it.' And they hid whatever there was. The fact that no more animals were killed for my sake was, I believe, thanks to the compassion of the Jowo himself." [KWGJ, f201]

Shabkar's decision to abstain from meat represented a considerable sacrifice. Although travelers in Tibet nowadays report that rice and vegetables imported from China can be found in many parts of the country, this was not the case in Shabkar's day. It is true that from time immemorial, in the low-lying regions to the south and east, enough grains and vegetables were grown for most of the population to supplement their essentially meat-based diet. But the cultivation of vegetables on a scale sufficient to provide what would now be regarded as an adequate vegetarian diet was impossible. No crops can grow at altitudes of over twelve thousand feet, and the north of Tibet is covered by immense grasslands suitable only for the raising of livestock: yaks, goats, and sheep. To give up eating meat was therefore a truly heroic act, accomplished by very few. It meant being satisfied with a diet consisting of little more than butter, curd, and *tsampa*, the traditional Tibetan flour made of roasted barley, usually eaten as lumps of dough mixed with butter and tea. It meant putting up with a reduced resistance to disease, the result of protein and vitamin deficiencies, and it surely meant a greater vulnerability to cold, felt much more keenly when one is deprived of an adequate intake of fat. It is understandable that such a diet was beyond the capacity of the majority. Even in a country where the principles of the Mahayana were omnipresent, where no one was ignorant of the Buddha's teachings on compassion, it was simply impossible for most people to live out such teachings on the level of their eating habits. In the case of the large monasteries, the provision for the monks of adequate supplies of vegetable food, even if they had been inclined to a meatless diet, was completely out of the question. To be a vegetarian in Tibet required powers of endurance and a determination that could only come from the deepest possible conviction.

All these considerations—the breadth of Shabkar's practice embracing the entire range of the Doctrine, his unconditional allegiance to all schools of Tibetan Buddhism, the perfect integrity of his own character, and the sacrifices he was prepared to make in order to live according to his insights and principles—give Shabkar an unusual authority and entitle him to speak for the whole of the tradition. What he has to say about meat eating and its relation to Buddhist practice is therefore important and should be heard, even if perhaps it diverges from our own views and preferences or seems beyond our powers.

Before considering Shabkar's arguments in greater detail, we should advert to the difficulty, perhaps impossibility, of arriving at a definition of the Buddhist teaching on meat eating such as to command assent from all sides. The most obvious reason for this is that the Buddha's own attitude toward meat eating, as presented in the scriptures, appears ambiguous. In some sutras, specifically those of the Hinayana, we find the Buddha advising his disciples to abstain from only certain kinds of meat, thereby implying that meat as such is an acceptable food. He also allows the ordained sangha to eat meat subject to certain conditions. On other occasions, the Buddha is said to have eaten meat himself, and the claim has been made, though not without contestation, that his death was occasioned by the consumption of an offering of infected pork.[9] Elsewhere, notably in the *Lankavatara-sutra* and other Mahayana scriptures, the Buddha criticizes the eating of meat in the strongest terms and forbids it under all circumstances. Finally, in certain texts of the Secret Mantra, the consumption of meat, along with alcohol, seems to be not merely allowed but actually advocated.

Shabkar approaches this conundrum in the spirit of the gradual path and explains the apparent contradictions of the scriptures as manifestations of the Buddha's pedagogical skill. Having attained enlightenment for himself, the Buddha did not seek to demonstrate his own greatness by proclaiming sublime truths into the void, beyond the reach of his audience. His first wish was to bring others to his own level of understanding, and in this he was a pragmatist. Knowing that people are transformed only by what they can understand and actually assimilate, he did not mystify them with subtle and abstruse words or try to impose on them disciplines that were beyond their strength. Instead, he spoke to them according to their ability and need.

The teachings recorded in the scriptures are therefore circumstantial, bestowed in a given situation and to specific individuals. A teaching appropriate for one person or group of persons is not necessarily suitable for others. Instructions intended for disciples of great acuity, and that approximate more closely the Buddha's own understanding, are not appropriate for disciples of more modest capacity, who need a more gradual approach. Buddhist scriptures present an entire spectrum of instruction, all of which has a single aim: to lead beings to liberation.

Two important conclusions follow from this. The first is that there exists a hierarchy of teaching, a scale of validity, according to which basic instruction is regarded as provisional, set forth according to need and superseded by higher, more demanding instruction to be expounded when the disciple is ready. For Shabkar, as for all teachers of Tibetan Buddhism, the instructions set forth on the Hinayana level are of vital importance in laying the foundations for correct understanding and practice. But they are not final. They are surpassed by the teachings of the Mahayana, just as, within the Mahayana itself, the sutra teachings prepare the way for, and are surpassed by, the tantra. It is thus that the entire sweep of the Buddha's teaching fits together in a harmonious and coherent system, in which teachings that seem incomplete from the standpoint of a higher view are assigned an appropriate, preparatory position lower down the scale. Viewed in this light, the teachings of both the Hinayana and Mahayana scriptures may be reconciled, and it is unnecessary to speculate, as some authorities have done, about the possibility of interpolated texts and the willful misrepresentation of the Buddha's words by later generations.[10]

The second important conclusion is that the validity of a given teaching depends on the circumstances in which it was imparted. It is a mistake to quote teachings out of context, applying them too broadly, in situations for which they were not designed. Thus an instruction given in a Hinayana setting is out of place, and does not retain the same validity, in a Mahayana context. As Shabkar demonstrates, it is owing to a superficial and incorrect reading of scripture that much of the confusion about meat eating has arisen.

As we have seen, despite the presence of the Mahayana in Tibet, and of great masters who expounded and lived it in all its purity, its implementation on the point of meat eating was not a practical option for most people. And as we have already suggested, the use of scripture quoted out of context to justify the consumption of meat is part of a very human scenario. When people are constrained by weakness to act in a manner that is at variance with their ideals, it is natural for them, whether to save face or simply to alleviate the resulting psychological pressure, to try to rationalize their behavior and justify it. In situations of genuine difficulty, it is also natural to follow the line of least resistance. For example, in Kham or Amdo at the winter's end, everyone is intensely hungry. If meat is available, it would be a hard heart indeed that would criticize or even question those who buy and consume it without worrying overmuch about how it has been procured, telling themselves that they are not responsible for the animal's death.

But no matter how cogent the circumstantial argument may be, and there is little doubt that it was and is so in Tibet, it is still important to preserve the essential principle. However much the eating of meat may be justified in the case of given individuals and circumstances, this should not be allowed to obscure the basic fact that meat eating does violence to the Mahayana ideal and is in normal circumstances indefensible. It is clear from Shabkar's writings that this was one of his main preoccupations: However difficult the practical conditions are, it is necessary to proclaim the truth and to keep the ideal alive. All this serves to throw Shabkar's position into even sharper relief. His teaching on the consumption of meat appears extraordinary and idealistic even in the affluent West; how much more so in the harsh conditions of Tibet.

Still, the fact remains that there are no inflexible rules. Whatever the geographical and cultural environment, behavior is a matter of individual capacity and choice. It is obvious that informed sincerity is the most important factor, although it must be admitted that, where judgment is liable to be swayed by desire and the strength of habit, self-deception can be a tenacious companion.

Shabkar was perfectly aware of these complicating factors, and his attitude was one of compassionate realism. He deplored the objective situation, but he knew very well that he was advocating a practice that was out of reach for many of his fellow Tibetans. He advocated it all the same but without being moralistic or judgmental. He grieved for the victims of the butchers, and he was impatient at the hypocrisy and sophistry of certain established practices. But he knew that in the circumstances—perhaps any circumstances—the best way to improve the situation was by persuasion and example.

The first part of his autobiography concludes with a verse in which he reviews his exploits so far, that is, up to the age of fifty-six. Speaking for himself, he says, "I kept all the Pratimoksha vows, the Bodhisattva vows, and those of the Mantrayana. I gave up meat, alcohol, garlic, onion, and tobacco, and sustained myself on the three whites, on the three sweets,[11] on tea and butter and tsampa." [KWGJ, f480b] He then mentions his disciples: his 108 great spiritual sons, the 1,800 great meditators, both men and women, the tens of thousands of monks and nuns who were his followers living in the monasteries, and the countless yogis, village practitioners, and devoted householders who did what they could in the practice, by prayers, fasting, and recitation of mantra. Of this immense following, he singles out for special mention those practitioners who, "having attained perfect loving-kindness, compassion, and bodhichitta, gave up eating meat."

[KWGJ, f480b] There were about three hundred of them—a tiny proportion, which he mentions nevertheless with delighted appreciation.

The rest of Shabkar's disciples were meat eaters—whom he accepted as students to be trained on the path. In *The Faults of Eating Meat*, Shabkar quotes the *Mahaparinirvana-sutra,* in which the Buddha says, "My teaching is not like that of the naked ascetics. I, the Tathagata, established rules of discipline in relation to specific individuals." Following in the same tradition, Shabkar was not an intolerant fundamentalist, advocating a single rule in all circumstances. His concern was that people should change and grow. For us who follow the path, faced as we are with objectives that are, for the moment, beyond us, to adopt a humble attitude and to be prepared to "start where we are" using the raw material of our personality as we find it, with all its needs and weaknesses, is the most— indeed the only—realistic approach. If, for whatever reason, we cannot do without meat, then it is as meat eaters that we begin to train. And the fact that we are training and progressing toward a goal is the very reason it is so necessary to respect the ideal and not obscure it with specious arguments. The acceptance of the possibility of change is a precondition for moral progress. In following the way of the Bodhisattvas, one must expect to be transformed; and given the depth and extent of that transformation, the possible modification of one's diet might well seem only a minor adjustment.

THE HINAYANA AND THREEFOLD PURITY

Whatever opinions Buddhists of different traditions may entertain about the eating of meat, all are in agreement about one thing: It is evil to take life. The vow to abstain from killing is the first Buddhist precept, and the very fact of becoming a Buddhist, by taking refuge in the Three Jewels, automatically involves the commitment not to inflict harm on any sentient being. In addition, Buddhists agree that, in ordinary circumstances, the taking of life also plants the seed of suffering in the mindstream of the perpetrator. Now it is obvious that the availability of meat involves the death of the animal it came from; and if the animal concerned has been killed, as opposed to dying from natural causes, the question is whether the karmic consequences of the killing are transferred to, or in any way shared by, the eater of the meat. Perhaps concern about this question was one reason the Buddha enunciated the principle of threefold purity. According to this teaching, it is possible to eat meat without sharing in the fault of the killer if one has not seen, has not heard, and has no suspicion that the animal in question has been killed for the express purpose of providing oneself with food. Conversely, to eat meat while knowing that the animal in question has been killed for one's own nourishment establishes a complicity with the killer and a share in the act. It generates a negative karma commensurate with the killing itself. The principle of threefold purity was, like many of Buddha's disciplinary directives, dictated by circumstances—in the present case, that of wandering monks receiving their daily food by almsgiving.[12] This practice, still followed by the Theravada monks in Thailand and elsewhere, is carried out according to a simple and beautiful ritual, normally in an atmosphere of complete anonymity. Leaving their forest *vihara*s as soon as it is light enough to see their way, the monks arrive at the entrance to the village where the devoted lay people place in their bowls a share of the food, whatever it may be, that they themselves will eat later on. No word is spoken. The monks signify their gratitude by bowing and then walk away. There is no sense of mundane conviviality, no discussion of the origin of the food. The monks are then expected to eat mindfully the contents of their bowls, good or bad, delicious or revolting, accepting whatever comes their way in a spirit of detachment.

In addition to being evil in itself, the act of killing, or causing another to kill, constitutes, for the sangha, a root violation that entails the destruction of monastic ordination. For monks and nuns, it is thus a matter of some importance whether the acceptance of a food offering containing meat involves complicity with the killer. The principle of threefold purity was thus intended to specify the occasions when the monks could eat meat—should it ever appear in their begging bowls—without damaging their ordination. The preoccupation, in other words, is primarily with purity of discipline and the possible accumulation of negativity. The focus of interest is the monks themselves, who, in this Hinayana context of Pratimoksha, are chiefly concerned with the task of self-liberation from the round of suffering and, as an accessory to this, with the purity of their vows.

It is obvious that in cultural settings other than the one just mentioned, meat endowed with threefold purity is practically impossible to find. It may well be that the forest monks remain completely unaware of the origin of their food, or they may quite reasonably assume that what is placed in their bowls on a daily basis forms part of the standard fare of the donors and that if scraps of meat appear in their bowls, they are part of what the villagers have either killed or bought for themselves. Outside this very specific milieu, the circumstances and their moral implications are naturally very different. The religious institutions of Tibet are a world away from the forest hermitages of India and south Asia. Tibetan monasteries were often immense, and many were located in remote, sparsely populated regions. Provisions were required on a large scale and had to be purchased and transported. This, as Shabkar observes, implies commerce and the market forces of supply and demand. And wherever there is a market, be it a Himalayan bazaar or a local supermarket in Europe or America, the possibility of three-fold purity is ruled out. In discussing it, Shabkar's intention was to place it in its proper context and to show that it could not be invoked to justify the eating of meat by Tibetan monks. The purpose of the principle was to isolate the only kind of meat the consumption of which did not impair the Pratimoksha ordination. On the other hand, the large-scale provision of "pure" meat is, practically speaking, a contradiction in terms. However unavoidable the eating of meat may be in Tibet, it is illegitimate to appeal to such a principle in order to defend and normalize it.

For those who were able and willing, abstention from meat in the harsh climate of Tibet implied a readiness to live practically on the brink of starvation. Such a lifestyle was obviously not for the majority. Yet Shabkar was not an isolated case. In the earliest period of Buddhism in Tibet, abstinence from meat in the monasteries must have been the norm, as can be seen from the legislation of King Trisong Detsen (a fact that Shabkar mentions in another of his works).[13] Admittedly, the monastic institutions at that time must have been much smaller and less numerous than they were to become. They also enjoyed royal patronage and so were well provided for. But in any case, at all times in Tibetan history, there have been famous masters, and no doubt a proportion of their disciples, who abstained from meat. Many of the Kadampas did so, beginning with Atisha himself, and they were followed by masters and practitioners of all schools—Milarepa, Drikung Kyobpa, Taklung Thangpa, Phagmo Drupa, Thogme Zangpo, Drukpa Kunleg, and so on, down to masters of more modern times like Jigme Lingpa, Nyakla Pema Dudul, and Patrul Rinpoche. In the case of Patrul Rinpoche, the celebrated author of *The Words of My Perfect Teacher*, it is well known that, through his incessant exposition of the *Bodhicharyavatara* and his repeated teachings on the helpless plight of animals, he effectively abolished, in many parts of eastern Tibet, the practice of slaughtering animals and offering their meat to visiting lamas.[14]

MEAT EATING AND THE MAHAYANA

The principle of threefold purity was set forth in the context of the Hinayana teachings as a guideline to ensure the integrity of the Pratimoksha vows. In the Mahayana, there is a profound change of emphasis: from the wish to free oneself from suffering to an intense awareness of the suffering of all beings and the cultivation of the wish to protect and liberate them. Since the ability to free others implies the achievement of freedom also for oneself, the Hinayana is by no means rejected; it is the basis of the Mahayana and is incorporated and transfigured by it. The need for "self-liberation" is acknowledged, but the shift of emphasis is toward "other-liberation," or, to be more exact, to a state of wisdom in which the distinction between self and other is seen to be unreal and is transcended.

It is important to reflect and dwell upon this polarity of self and other. It is an axiom of Buddhist doctrine that all living beings without exception experience the impression of being "I," of having a self to which they cling. They serve the interests of this imagined self, and they fear and resist anything that menaces it. They want to be happy; they do not want to suffer. This fundamental desire, rooted as it is in self-clinging, is the basis not only of personal existence but also of the spiritual quest. Like everyone else, practitioners on the Hinayana level are also striving for happiness, the definitive happiness of nirvana. The wish for individual liberation, of liberation for oneself, is perfectly in line with the same fundamental urge that in less skillful beings results in samsara. It is a mark of the Buddha's pedagogical genius that the basic impetus of self-interest is utilized as the energy source that impels the trainee beyond samsara and the self-clinging that is its cause. As the Dalai Lama often says, we are self-centered beings; the Buddha has taught us how to be wisely self-centered. With this in mind, we can appreciate why the training on the Hinayana level is in the nature of a disciplinary restriction. The energies that, uncontrolled, result in the futile sufferings of samsara are bound by vows; they are channeled and utilized to good effect. One learns to abandon negativity and to adopt the skillful techniques of discipline, concentration, and wisdom, according to the direction of one's original impetus: the desire for one's own happiness.

By contrast, there is in the Mahayana something that goes against the grain. Honest self-scrutiny reveals that we are not naturally selfless, that is, concerned for others to the detriment of our own interests. Altruism takes us beyond ourselves and is something that we must consciously learn. It is moreover a matter of experience that in order to feel commitment to any kind of training, it is necessary to be inspired and to have a longing for the goals to be achieved. This is why, in the *Bodhicharyavatara*, a distinction is made between bodhichitta of aspiration—the interest and wish to attain complete enlightenment for the sake of others—and bodhichitta in action—the actual engagement and practice of the Bodhisattva path that brings about such a goal.

As the teachings explain,[15] these two facets of bodhichitta are associated with different vows and disciplines, and at the beginning of *The Nectar of Immortality*, Shabkar mentions two practices that are specifically associated with bodhichitta in aspiration. The first is the famous seven-stage instruction, designed to create a feeling of closeness with others. This is based on the understanding that all beings have, at some moment in their samsaric career, been linked to us in a parent-child relationship. The object of the exercise is to come to the recognition that all beings, in whatever shape or form they happen to be now, have at some point been close to us and have loved us deeply. They have cherished us and protected us, and we have been precious to them. It is the ever-repeated tragedy of our samsaric condition that we have completely forgotten those who once cherished us, just as we are soon to forget those—wife, husband, lover, parents, children—who are dear to us in our present existence. The conclusion we are to draw from such thoughts is that all beings, human and animal, friend and foe, known and unknown—all are our long-lost loved ones.

The second of the techniques associated with bodhichitta in aspiration is the practice of "equality and exchange." This is expounded at length by Shantideva in the *Bodhicharyavatara* and is a more philosophical approach. It uses logical reflection to undermine the seemingly watertight distinction between self and other, showing that these are conceptual constructs without intrinsic validity—no more real than optical illusions.[16] These two techniques work well together. The practice of equality and exchange creates the right mental environment, demonstrating that compassion is essentially reasonable. By contrast, the seven-stage instruction has a much more emotional appeal and is designed to create an unbearable sense of the closeness of other beings and of their suffering, so that the mind is galvanized with the wish, in fact the decision, to do something to relieve and liberate them. When both understanding and feeling have been developed and brought to a sufficient pitch of intensity, genuine compassion becomes possible. Once again, it should be stressed that these two trainings form part of the commitments associated with bodhichitta *in aspiration*. It is only when they are perfected that genuine bodhichitta arises in the mind. This does not of course mean that one must wait for these trainings to be complete before engaging in the activities associated with bodhichitta in action (generosity and the other paramitas). On the other hand, the later trainings will not be complete until the earlier trainings have achieved their purpose.

The trainings associated with aspirational bodhichitta are therefore the very foundation of Mahayana practice, and that Shabkar should mention them at the opening of his work is not at all unusual. What is striking is the connection he makes between these trainings and the consumption of meat. For he actually says that when these mental disciplines have been perfected—when, for instance, one has a vivid sense that all beings have been as kind and close to us as our own dear parents—it becomes literally impossible to feed upon their flesh. By contrast, the taking of meat, regarded as an ordinary food and eaten unreflectively on a regular basis, implies an unawareness and an indifference to the suffering of beings that is incompatible with the mind training. The continued craving for meat and the satisfaction of this craving may thus be taken as a sign that the training in aspirational bodhichitta is not yet perfect. To this it must be added that, in adopting this position, Shabkar is focusing not upon meat as such but upon the beings that have been tormented and killed in order to make meat available. It follows that his censure covers not only the consumption of meat as food but the use of all products the procuring of which has involved the killing and abuse of animals.

For many of us, perhaps, this teaching is difficult to accept. It suggests that however long we have been practicing Dharma, our desire for and consumption of meat and animal products indicates that we are no more than beginners on the Mahayana path. We will return to this point, but as a preparation for the reading of Shabkar, it may be helpful to consider a little further the basic orientation of the Mahayana, which explains and gives legitimacy to Shabkar's position.

In addition to training in the two disciplines mentioned above, aspirants on the Bodhisattva path are encouraged to cultivate four "boundless" attitudes, so called because their field of action (all sentient beings) and the resulting merit are incalculably vast. These attitudes are love (the sincere wish that others be happy), compassion (the sincere wish that others not suffer), sympathetic joy (a heartfelt rejoicing in the good fortune of others), and impartiality (the ability to apply the previous three attitudes to all beings without differentiation).

Of these four attitudes, the fourth is the most significant and challenging.

When we survey the world from the apparently central position that we ourselves occupy, we find that the aggregate of living beings falls into three categories. First, there are those who seem close to us, who appear beautiful, attractive, good, and important. Then there are those whom we dislike or fear and who seem distant, menacing, and bad. Finally, between these two extremes, there is the vast multitude of beings whom we simply do not know, who do not engage our interest, and with whom we are linked in a relation of indifference. To perceive matters in this way is part of what it means to be in samsara; it is the inescapable result of having a sense of self and of clinging to it. This division of the world into good, bad, and indifferent is such a deep-rooted instinct that we habitually take it for objective reality, yet it is no more than an illusion created by our own self-clinging. The truth is of course that no one is intrinsically pleasant, intrinsically bad, or intrinsically unimportant, and the practice of impartiality is intended to break down the sheer narrow-mindedness of such egocentric assumptions. For it is only when we call these ideas into question that we may achieve a glimpse of other beings separate from us, as it were *from their own side*, in a manner that is undistorted by our own self-centered attitudes and expectations. And we perceive, perhaps for the first time, that, quite independently of us and our relationship with them, they are all the same—all without exception, from our own dear children to the least significant (to us) insect. Everyone wants only one thing: to be happy and to avoid sorrow. All living beings, human or animal, wish for fulfillment according to the nature and scope of their present embodied state.

It is interesting to consider the extent to which this insight runs counter to our basic instincts. We naturally attach importance to whatever falls within the gravitational field of our own ego, to the detriment of what does not. We overlook those who are unfortunate enough to be outside our group, forgetting that in their one basic desire, all are alike. We have a built-in predilection for *our* family, *our* community, *our* tradition, *our* country, nation, race, and so on, and it seems natural to cultivate and defend them as our first duty, leaving the rest to their own devices. And to these categories must also be added *our* species. We think that only humans are important.

It is true that Buddhism attaches a supreme value to the human condition. It does so because it is in the human form alone that effective spiritual training and eventual liberation are possible. But apart from this, all beings—humans and animals both—are the same. They all cling to a sense of self and pursue their own interests, whether impelled by instinct or by conscious choice. When attacked, they all try to defend and save themselves. Given the chance, they seek fulfillment, according to their capacity and need, both for themselves and for those close to them. They try to avoid frustration. Clinging to the illusion of self, beings wander in samsara. They all—we all—suffer, and it is our suffering, not our existential status, that qualifies us as objects of compassion. *All* beings, not just human beings, are therefore the beneficiaries of the Buddha's enlightenment, and the liberation of them all is the goal of the Mahayana path. It is true that, on the whole, humans are more intelligent and resourceful than other species, and it is true, too, that, because of their spiritual potential, humans are not normally to be sacrificed for the sake of animals (although, in the case of highly realized Bodhisattvas this might occur, as with the earlier incarnation of Shakyamuni Buddha, who gave his body to feed a starving tigress). From the Buddhist point of view, on the other hand, it is a fallacy of theistic religion to suppose that Man has been made "Lord of creation" and that the other species have been provided for our use, our sustenance, and our amusement. Beings appear in the world according to their karma; they all have an equal right to be here. The realization of this fundamental truth is one of the aims of the practice of impartiality. It is the sympathetic appreciation of the predicament of all beings, human or otherwise, independent of our self-centered perspective, our interests, and our desires.

Once this basic notion has been grasped, the difference between the Mahayana and Hinayana approaches to meat eating is easy to understand. In the Mahayana, the object of concern is no longer the eater of the meat and the possibility of his or her defilement. Instead, it is the victim, the living being that dies in fear and pain so that its body can be consumed or used for some other purpose. This lies at the heart of Shabkar's thought and practice, and it surfaces again and again in his autobiography. He could not remain silent, haunted as he was by the torment of animals, hunted to their deaths, slaughtered by the thousand to provide food for those who could not or would not nourish themselves in any other way. Shabkar was of one mind with Patrul Rinpoche in acknowledging the obvious but ignored truth that, weak and stupid as animals may be, they do not want to die. And he lamented that their lives, their only possession, are taken from them by and for those who, in contravention of the principles of mind training, construct their happiness upon the misery of others.

If such was Shabkar's approach to the eating of meat in Tibet, it is not difficult to imagine his reaction to the situation, had he known it, of his fellow Tibetans in exile or of Buddhist practitioners in the affluent West, where the procurement of wholesome and delicious alternatives poses no real difficulty and where in so many ways the production of meat constitutes an immense, cruel, and utterly inhumane industry. Above all, he could not tolerate the perversion of the teachings, as he saw it, by those who sought to justify their practices by specious and self-serving rationalizations. He firmly dismissed the argument of threefold purity, first because it is out of place in a Mahayana context, and second because it was manifestly irrelevant in Tibet. He had little time for the ostensibly pious practices of praying for the animals, the real purpose of which was to salve the uneasy consciences of killer and consumer, and he strenuously objected to the idea that animals are benefited when their flesh is eaten by those who claim to be practitioners but who consume meat out of ordinary desire.

On the other hand, Shabkar recognized that there are always exceptions to the rule. He recognized too that the consumption of meat might, in exceptional circumstances, represent the better course—in cases of extreme need, for instance, when there is literally nothing else to eat, or when it is necessary to remedy the physical debility of aged masters whose passing away would greatly hinder the preservation of the teachings.

MEAT IN THE MANTRAYANA

The Mantrayana, the vehicle of skillful means whereby the objects of the senses are utilized on the path, is thought by many to allow and even to advocate the consumption of meat as well as alcohol. The texts certainly declare that, in the *ga-nachakra* offering, "meat and alcohol should not be lacking." In practice, this is often interpreted as meaning that the gana-chakra is an occasion to enjoy meat and wine, sometimes in large quantities, in the ordinary sense of the word—and as sanctioning their consumption on a day-to-day basis. The fact, however, that some of the greatest tantric masters in the history of Tibetan Buddhism abstained from meat at all times, and encouraged their disciples to do the same, suggests that the matter is less straightforward than it appears. The teaching of the tantras on the use of sense objects is very subtle and, as with all complex subjects, is easily misrepresented and misapplied.

Generally speaking, each of the three vehicles—the Hi-nayana and the sutra and tantra vehicles of the Mahayana—displays a characteristic orientation. The Hinayana is concerned with self-liberation. Its specific quality of mind is renunciation (*nges byung*), the definitive decision to leave sam-sara. Building on that determination, the Mahayana is concerned with bodhichitta, and its hallmarks are an altruistic concern for others and an understanding of the wisdom of emptiness. In the case of the Mantrayana, which is often referred to as the resultant vehicle because it takes as the path the enlightened qualities already implicit in the *tathagata-garbha*, or buddha-nature, the emphasis is on the realization of the primordial purity and equality of all phenomena. Here, the concepts of clean and unclean (a distinction deeply rooted in our psychological makeup and reflected and reinforced by our cultural setting), together with other dualistic pairings such as pain and pleasure, joy and sorrow, good and bad, and so on, have no meaning. They are regarded as self-centered illusions to be transcended. This explains the unconventional lifestyles of many of the great *siddhas* and tantric masters of the past. Living on the margins of society, they often appeared, and often behaved, in ways that ordinary people found disgusting if not actually horrific. Kukuripa, for example, lived among the dogs; Virupa nourished himself on the foul, glutinous entrails of rotting fish; while, in Tibet, the celebrated Tsangnyön Heruka once regaled himself with putrid, maggot-infested brain matter taken from some decapitated heads he found hanging on a city gate.[17] Such figures have also been an important, if exceptional, feature of tantric Buddhism right up to modern times.

The overcoming of the dualistic concepts of purity and impurity is one reason meat and alcohol, normally regarded in a Buddhist context as unclean or reprehensible, are demanded as ingredients for tantric practice. In stipulating their presence at the ganachakra, the scriptures and *sadhana* instructions prescribe elements—the five meats and five nectars—that ordinary practitioners of the Mahayana, or anyone else for that matter, might be expected to find impure, unacceptable, or even repellent. The ganachakra is never to be understood as a pretext for ordinary indulgence. The Dalai Lama has observed, "In this regard, someone might try to justify eating meat on the grounds that he or she is a practitioner of Highest Yoga Tantra. But this person must not forget that included in the five nectars and five meats are substances that are normally considered dirty and repulsive. A true practitioner of Highest Yoga Tantra does not discriminate by taking the meat but not the dirty substances. But we cover our noses if such dirty substances are anywhere near us, let alone actually ingesting them."[18] In view of all this, there is surely something ridiculous in ganachakra ceremonies where the yogis and yoginis dine on fillet of steak washed down with liberal drafts of Burgundy.

Practitioners who are able to enjoy the five meats and five nectars, or anything resembling them, in a state beyond duality are genuine tantrikas. To pretend otherwise—to use the ganachakra as a pretext for ordinary enjoyments—is at best to reduce the practice to the level of an empty ritual. On the other hand, even in the case of authentic yogis, the principle of "pure meat" is said to apply. At least in the case of practitioners who are unable to lead the consciousness of the dead to a buddhafield, the appropriate offering should come from an animal that has died a natural death. By contrast, to make a ganachakra offering of the good, fresh meat of an animal slaughtered for consumption is, according to Patrul Rinpoche, a complete aberration. It is like inviting the Buddhas and Bodhisattvas to a banquet and offering them the flesh of their own children.[19]

In answer to this, it may be argued that the meat and alcohol offered in the ganachakra are no longer ordinary. They are purified and transformed by the power of mantra. It is therefore permissible to enjoy them. This, however, is true only when the people offering the ganachakra are accomplished beings who have realized the primordial purity and equality of all phenomena and for whom the offering substances really are transformed. It is only they, moreover, who are able to benefit the beings from whose bodies the meat has been taken.[20]

It is sometimes said, quoting from the tantras, that "the compassionate one eats meat; the holder of samaya drinks

alcohol." To this Shabkar replies, "If this is the case, since
the Buddha and his Shravakas, the six ornaments and the two
supreme ones of India,[21] Atisha and his spiritual sons, and all
the other holy beings consumed neither meat nor alcohol,
one is forced to conclude either that they were without compassion and had not been observing samaya, or that their
compassion was less than that of the people who put forward
this objection."[22] In other words, the literal exegesis of the
text in question cannot be seriously entertained. It would be
more reasonable to regard the quotation as an example of
"indirect teachings expressed in metaphors,"[23] on the same
level as the injunction to slay one's parents and assassinate the
king. As Shabkar comments elsewhere, "When in the Secret
Mantra teachings it is said that one should eat meat, this is
not an explicit teaching. In the commentary to the tantra
mkha' 'gro rgya mtsho it is specified that the eating of meat
refers to the 'devouring of discursive thoughts.' "[24]

It is sometimes said that when practitioners of the
Dharma and especially of the Vajrayana eat meat, their actions
are justified because they are creating a connection between
the slaughtered animal and the teachings. They are conferring
a special benefit on the animal. It is therefore good to eat
meat, in quantity and on a regular basis. Shabkar considered
this line of reasoning particularly laughable. Like many false
but attractive arguments, it is constructed of half-truths. The
principle of interdependence, it is urged, is universally applicable and must of necessity be operative in the present case.
If it is possible to gain a connection with the Dharma by
seeing, hearing, or touching representations of the teaching,
it is logical to suppose that an animal gains a connection with
the teachings by being eaten by a Dharma practitioner. No

doubt there is some truth in this contention. But the question that must now be asked is whether the principle is universally applicable and whether, in particular, it is applicable to *us*. If, given interdependence, it is possible for an animal to be benefited through the consumption of its flesh, much will depend on the status of the consumer—on his or her own connection with the Dharma and on the degree of his or her spiritual attainment. If the person eating the meat is an enlightened being—a Buddha or a great Bodhisattva residing on the grounds of realization—it is not difficult to suppose that, compared with other animals slaughtered for their meat, the being in question is indeed fortunate. But honesty must surely oblige us to admit that, in our case—that of ordinary people, struggling with the practice—"connection with the Dharma" consists of listening to a few teachings, reading a few books, attending an empowerment or two, having the blessed substances placed upon our heads, and trying, when we have time and the mood takes us, to meditate and practice. When all is said and done, our own connection with the teachings is tenuous enough. And if it were ever to occur to us to wonder about the predicament of the being whose body we are in the process of eating, who of us would be able even to locate its mind in the bardo, let alone lead it to a buddhafield? What possible benefit could conceivably come to an animal by having its flesh eaten by the likes of us—mere aspirants on the path, who are without accomplishment and are ourselves prisoners of samsara?

Nevertheless, it must be admitted that, according to the principle of interdependence just mentioned, there are exceptional beings, far advanced along the spiritual path, with whom contact of any kind establishes a link with the teachings and is a source of great blessing. Accomplished masters and yogis do exist, capable of benefiting beings by eating their flesh. Shabkar of course was perfectly aware of this and warned his disciples to tread carefully in their regard and to abstain from all criticism. This question is discussed at length in *The Emanated Scripture of Pure Vision*, a text in which Shabkar departs from his usual emphasis on renunciation and lojong suited to most practitioners and discusses the use of sense pleasures and bliss, characteristic of the teachings of the Secret Mantra. He carefully describes the kind of people qualified to implement such techniques appropriately, without danger to themselves and others.

In relation to such beings, the ordinary person is on a knife edge, since it is a natural tendency to evaluate the character and actions of others and to compare them with oneself. In normal circumstances, such comparisons may not be out of place and may even be beneficial. But if one is foolish enough to measure oneself against an accomplished master and if one presumes to criticize him or her, the karmic consequences may be very serious.[25] In the colophon to *The Emanated Scripture of Pure Vision*, Shabkar remarks that on numerous occasions he had pondered the need for such a text, since he had noted, in the course of his travels, a general tendency to criticize certain Vajrayana practitioners for not renouncing meat, alcohol, and sex. And he remarks elsewhere that since as a rule one is unable to judge the spiritual level of others, it is better always to assume the best and to practice pure vision, refraining from any kind of criticism of people whose spiritual realization may be far in advance of one's own. Pure perception is in fact one of the cardinal features of the Vajrayana path. After explaining why the latter is generally a matter of secrecy, Shabkar concludes, "One must be careful to cultivate a pure perception of the activities of the Bodhisattvas and great Siddhas. On the other hand, simple and immature disciples should not recklessly try to imitate them."[26]

In the majority of cases, it is obvious that the argument that one is helping animals by eating them is absurd. In a long poem contained in his autobiography, Shabkar refers to the matter with ironic humor. He describes himself sitting in a meadow, surrounded by a large flock of sheep and goats. An old sheep comes forward and speaks to him, lamenting the terrible destiny of domestic animals, even in a religious country like Tibet.

> *The fate of goats and old mother ewes*
> *Lies in the hands of visiting lamas.*
> *Now, in the bardo, and in our future lives,*
> *The guru is our only hope,*
> *So pity us.*
> *Do not now betray us in this time of hope!*

> *Let us live our lives out to the end,*
> *Or take us, when we die, to higher realms.*
> *If you do not do so,*
> *Pain will be our lot in this and future lives.*
> *From one life to the next we're killed and killed again.*
> *Do not let your wisdom, love, and power be so feeble!*
> *. . . . .*
> *Patrons come to you the lamas, cap in hand.*
> *"Visit us, come to our house," they say.*
> *But don't pretend you do not know*

That as they're greeting you,
It's us the sheep they're planning to dispatch!

. . . .

When the lama comes into the house
And takes his seat upon his comfy throne,
They're killing us outside, just by the door!
Don't pretend you do not know,
You who are omniscient!

Shabkar replies with the standard argument. Throughout
the animals' past lives, not once have they been able to con-
tribute something to the preservation of the Doctrine. They
should now be glad at such an opportunity! By relinquishing
their bodies to nourish the lama, they are doing something
worthwhile. "Is it not a noble thing," Shabkar exclaims, "to
give up one's body for the Dharma?" But it is the animals
themselves who are given the last word. "As I said that, the
goats and sheep exclaimed with one voice: 'Oh, no! He is
one of *those* lamas!' And terrified, they all ran away." [KWGJ,
f167–168b]

The idea that one shows compassion to beings by feeding
on their flesh is certainly a strange one. Few would deny that
if *we* were given the choice of receiving a connection with
Dharma at the price of being devoured, there is not much
doubt that Dharma would be something we would happily
forgo. It is not difficult to see that the use of such an argument is not at all expressive of a genuine concern for animals;
it is a piece of self-serving sophistry, used to mask a very
ordinary desire. If one really were concerned about animals
and wished to give them a connection with the Dharma, it
would surely be more rational and more effective to buy them

from the butchers and set them free in their natural environment, after giving them blessed substances to eat and so on.

Finally, there is another argument sometimes adduced, this time in the attempt to weaken the position of those who advocate abstention from meat. It is that the production of all foods, including vegetables and cereals, involves the death of sentient beings. Many insects and small animals are killed in the cultivation of crops and the preparation of nonmeat foods, so what is the difference between vegetarian and meat-based diets? At first sight, there seems to be some validity in this point of view, since it is undeniable that enormous numbers of insects do die, especially given modern farming methods. A moment's reflection will show, however, that the argument is false both in principle and in practice. Compassion and the desire to protect from suffering—inner qualities essential to the Buddhist outlook—are grounded first and foremost in intention. Now the voluntary killing of animals is intrinsic to the production of meat; no meat can be made available otherwise. This on the other hand is not true of the cultivation of crops, where the destruction of sentient life, however great, is not intrinsic to the production of the crops themselves. It is brought about, or at least greatly aggravated, for motives of efficiency and profit. Any gardener knows that it is possible to grow vegetables without destroying insects *except by accident*. The consumption of vegetables therefore does not automatically involve the wish that others perish. But how can anyone possibly consume meat while sincerely wishing that the animal in question remain alive? In any case, this same argument, which is used to make vegetarianism seem irrational and ridiculous, cannot be adduced without undermining the position of its proponents. For it is well known that the raising of beef cattle, for instance, itself requires enormous quantities of grain, with the consequent loss of insect life that is superadded to the deaths of the livestock in question. Thus vegetarianism once again emerges as an effective means of reducing the slaughter!

CONCLUSION

For many of us, even committed Buddhists of long standing, Shabkar's words will seem a hard teaching. From childhood we are used to eating meat and making use of all sorts of other animal products. We belong to a society where the consumption of meat is encouraged and regarded as normal. Finally, we all enjoy delicious food, and our culinary traditions are such that our taste for meat is certainly no weaker than that of the Tibetans. It is surely a good deal stronger, given the variety and succulence of meat dishes available in our wealthy society. Furthermore, we may sincerely find that it is physically difficult, perhaps too difficult, to do without meat and fish; and perhaps socially, given our family and professional situations, a radical change of diet is for all intents and purposes out of the question. At the same time, we find that many of the arguments and practices commonly used to justify meat eating or to attenuate a sense of guilt, and which we might have used to quiet our uneasy consciences, are demolished by Shabkar, who shows them to be either untenable or just silly. So, given the sincerity and truth of Shabkar's teachings, how are we to assimilate and live by them, according to our capacity and circumstances?

The essential point to remember is that, as a Buddhist teacher, Shabkar, like the Buddha himself, aims only to draw

beings on the path and to help them to progress toward freedom and enlightenment. *Progress* is the operative word. Although Buddhist teachings do not hesitate to point out the
karmic consequences of actions and to issue the appropriate
warnings, the imposition of a rigid morality, to be embraced
come what may, by denying and repressing old habits and
needs, is foreign to the Buddhist spirit and is in any case
usually a hopeless enterprise. Instead, the Dharma is often
described as a medicine—a therapy—whereby bad habits and
perceived needs are examined and transformed from within.
Techniques are applied according to one's ability and situation, above all, gradually, so that the teachings are seen not as
a series of burdensome injunctions but as steps toward the
acquisition of inner freedom. The aim is not to repress one's
desire for meat or to terminate one's use of animal products
by a draconian act of will. Instead, our task is to develop a
heartfelt compassion and a genuine sensitivity to the suffering
of animals, such that the desire to exploit and feed on them
naturally dissolves. Shabkar's main concern is not to instill a
sense of guilt or inadequacy; it is to elevate the mind toward
new and more noble objectives.

In the immediate term, it may be very difficult for us to
give up meat or to forgo commodities (leather, detergents,
cosmetics, and so on) that are manufactured with methods
involving the abuse and torment of animals. But even when it
is impossible to abstain, there is still a great deal that we can
do to ameliorate the karmic situation and to dispose the mind
so that, when the opportunity eventually presents itself,
change is possible and even easy.

The first and perhaps the most important task is to make
an effort to remember what the consumption of meat implies.

It is a willingness to look beyond the mendacious publicity of the food industry, which does everything to conceal, behind a façade of aesthetic or sentimental advertisements (fluffy lambs, cartoon chickens), the horrific realities of the factory farm and the slaughterhouse—all of which exist for one reason only: that we may be well supplied with abundant and inexpensive meat. Many of us eat meat, but few of us would have the stomach to visit the places where our food is prepared—to witness not only the terror and agony of the animals transported, selected, and killed in their thousands on a daily basis but also the dreadful callousness and brutality of their butchers, who in providing us with meat are working on our behalf.

Alas, need and desire make us easy victims of deception and pretense. Yet it is precisely here, on the level of our daily sustenance, that the principles of the mind-training teachings are most easily neglected and betrayed. To forget where one's food has come from, to be careless of how it has been produced and at what cost, to eat insensitively, consuming meat in a routine manner without a moment's thought of the suffering involved, is to turn away from beings. It is to abandon them in a vast, anonymous ocean of suffering. How can this be compatible with the teaching of the Buddha?

Of course, it may be just too difficult for us to avoid eating meat or using animal products, but if such is the case, even the experience of regret and the desire that the situation be other than it is are themselves significant and of immense value. They are a step in the right direction. It takes courage to acknowledge a principle and an ideal even when one is unable to live by it, and yet it is this very acknowledgment that opens the door to change and progress. The rest follows gradually, according to one's possibilities. One may for whatever reason—physical need, social situation, or the strength of one's craving—be unable to give up meat, but it may be possible to reduce the amount one eats or to select the kind of meat that entails the least loss of life. The same principle applies to those who manage to abstain from meat completely but who find it too difficult, for the moment, to do without fur for their coats, leather for their shoes, certain kinds of soap, and so forth. Above all, it is precisely by cultivating a tender conscience, rather than dulling it with specious casuistry, that moral progress is made possible. Eventually, we may arrive at the point where our bodily needs and our way of living cease to be a source of terror and pain for other living beings.

Shabkar's convictions and feelings forced him to exhort others and to encourage them to the actual practice of compassion for all beings, humans and animals alike. But he realistically accepted that, at least in Tibet, he was speaking to a minority. "It is quite possible," he writes, "that no one can or will heed me. On the other hand, one or two intelligent and compassionate people might. So for their sake I must set this teaching forth to the best of my ability and wits."[27]

Toward the end of Shabkar's life, Patrul Rinpoche, moved by the stories he had heard, made the long journey from Kham to Amdo in order to meet him. He had gone only halfway when he received the news that Shabkar had died. He made a hundred prostrations in the direction of Amdo and sang a prayerful supplication for Shabkar's swift rebirth. "Compassion and love," he exclaimed, "are the roots of Dharma. I think that in the whole world, there is no one more compassionate than Lama Shabkar. I had nothing spe-

cial to ask him, no teachings to request, and none to offer. I
wanted only to gather some merit by gazing upon his face."[28]

Although Shabkar discusses the question of meat consumption in several of his writings,[29] the two texts translated here
are of particular interest. The first is an excerpt from *The
Wondrous Emanated Scripture,*[30] dealing with the faults of meat
eating (*sha'i nyes dmigs*), and for the most part it consists of
quotations, some quite extensive, from the Mahayana scriptures and the teachings of masters of all schools of Tibetan
Buddhism. Aside from the inspiring nature of the quotations
themselves, the collection is of interest because it shows that,
contrary to commonly held opinion, the condemnation of
meat eating is not an exclusive feature of the sutras. It is also
to be found in the tantras, including the highest tantras of the
anuttarayoga level. The second text, *The Nectar of Immortality,*[31] is a fully developed discourse in its own right. It is
Shabkar's most powerful and concentrated statement on the
subject and constitutes what must rank as one of the most
impassioned indictments of meat eating to be found in Tibetan literature. This text was recently rediscovered, in manu-
script form, by Matthieu Ricard in the course of a visit to
Amdo in 2001. It was found in a monastery in the Shophon
Valley, not far from Rekong where many yogis and practitioners of Shabkar's lineage still live. The text was lent for
copying by Yundrung Gyal, the nephew of the famous scholar
Gendun Chöpel. We are profoundly grateful to both Yundrung Gyal and Matthieu Ricard for sending the text to us.

These texts were translated by Helena Blankleder and
Wulstan Fletcher of the Padmakara Translation Group. We
would like to express our deep gratitude to Alak Zenkar

Rinpoche, Pema Wangyal Rinpoche, Jigme Khyentse Rinpoche, and Jetsün Yangchen Chödzom for their encouragement and help with the texts. We are also very grateful to Jenny Kane, Pamela Law, and Ingrid and Dolma Gunther for their suggestions and assistance.

The Faults
of Eating Meat

It is recorded in the *Lankavatara-sutra*:

AFTER THE GREAT BODHISATTVA Mahamati had recited
certain verses before the Lord, he made the following request:

"Lord and Tathagata, Foe-Destroyer[1] and Perfect Buddha,
I pray you, tell me how I and other Bodhisattva Mahasattvas
of the present time and in the future may remove the desire
for the taste of meat in those who are soiled by the habit of
consuming the flesh and blood of sentient beings. I beseech
you, Lord, set forth the teaching so that they may perceive
the wrongfulness of consuming meat, and that, longing instead for the taste of Dharma, they may cultivate the kind of
love that embraces all beings, cherishing them as their own
dear children. Explain your doctrine so that, filled with love,
they may progress upon the grounds of realization of the
Bodhisattvas and come swiftly to enlightenment, perfect and

unsurpassed, or, failing this, to refreshment in the state of Shravakas and Pratyekabuddhas, thence to progress to the un-surpassable state of Buddhahood. Lord, even those who fol-low not the Dharma but uphold false doctrines, falling to the extreme positions of existence or nonexistence, propounding an eternal entity or the nihilistic void of the materialists— even they proscribe the eating of meat. Even they abstain from it! But you, Lord, Protector of the World, you teach a doctrine that is flavored with compassion. It is the teaching of the perfect Buddhas. And yet we eat meat nonetheless; we have not put an end to it. Therefore, that I and the other great Bodhisattvas may set forth your doctrine as it is indeed, I entreat you, reveal the faults of consuming meat in the name of that compassion with which you regard all the beings in the world with an equal love."

The Lord answered, "Mahamati, listen carefully and re-member what I say. For excellent is your request, and I will teach you."

And the Bodhisattva, the great being Mahamati, listened attentively to the Lord, who said:

"Mahamati," he said, "a loving and compassionate Bo-dhisattva should not eat meat. There are countless reasons for this, only some of which I will explain to you. It is not easy, Mahamati, to come upon a being who, in the endless ages of samsara, has not been once your father or your mother, your brother or your sister, your son or daughter, kinsman, friend, or close companion. Your kith and kin in one existence, they have donned a different shape in later lives. They have be-come animals, wild or tame, beast or bird. Bodhisattva, great being Mahamati, all those who have faith in Buddha Dharma, those who wish to follow in my footsteps—how could they consume the flesh of living beings? Mahamati, when they hear the perfect Dharma of the Tathagatas, even demons keep from eating flesh; they turn from their demonic nature and begin to be compassionate. Is there any need therefore for me to mention those who have true faith in Dharma? Mahamati, since Bodhisattvas look upon all beings, the friends and close ones of their former lives, as their dearest children, they must shy away from every type of meat. It is unfitting, it is wrong, Mahamati, for those engaged upon the Bodhisattva path to partake of meat. Therefore they should abstain from it. Ordinary, worldly people naturally refrain from the flesh of donkeys, camels, dogs, elephants, and humans (though butchers, in order to enrich themselves, claim that it is edible and hawk it in the streets). It follows naturally that Bodhisattvas should refrain from meat of every kind. Mahamati, Bodhisattvas who wish to live pure lives should shrink from meat, for it is but the outcome of the male and female essential fluids.[2]

"Moreover, Mahamati, Bodhisattvas, who cherish all that lives, should keep from eating meat, for they do not wish to frighten beings, those endowed with physical form. O Mahamati, dogs are filled with terror, even at a distance, on catching sight of outcasts such as butchers, fishermen, and hunters—all of whom devour the flesh of dogs. Thinking that such people are coming to kill them, they almost die of fear. And likewise, Mahamati, when the small animals that live upon the earth or in the air and water see, even from afar, and detect with their keen sense of smell anyone who eats meat, they flee at once as quickly as a man might run from a cannibal for fear of being killed. Therefore, Mahamati, that they might not become a source of terror, Bodhisattvas, who abide in love, should not partake of meat. Ordinary beings, Mahamati, those who are not Aryas,[3] have an evil smell deriving from the meat that they consume. They thus become repulsive. But Aryas forsake such food completely, and therefore Bodhisattvas likewise should refrain from meat. The Aryas, O Mahamati, eat the food of sages; they abstain from meat and blood, and Bodhisattvas too should do as much.

"Mahamati, a compassionate Bodhisattva, wishing not to scandalize the people who might then decry my teaching, should eat no meat of any kind. This is how it is, O Mahamati. Some people in the world have criticized my doctrine, saying, 'Alas, what kind of virtue is it that these people practice? They do not live pure lives. They have abandoned what the wise of old once ate, and now they fill their bellies with the flesh of beasts, bringing fear to animals that live in air or water or upon the earth! They wander through the world; their virtuous practice has declined; they do not turn from evil ways. They are destitute of spiritual teachings and devoid of discipline!' Thus these people angrily decry my doctrine in many different ways. Therefore, Mahamati, a compassionate Bodhisattva, wishing not to scandalize the people so that they disdain my teaching, should not partake of meat of any kind.

"Bodhisattvas should refrain from meat. The smell of meat, O Mahamati, is no different from the stink of corpses. Between the stench of the burning flesh of corpses and the burned flesh of a beast there is no difference. Both are equally revolting. This is yet another reason a Bodhisattva on the path, who wishes for a life of purity, should not eat meat of any kind. Likewise, Mahamati, yogis living in the charnel grounds and in the spirit-haunted wilds, practitioners who live in solitude, and all who meditate on loving kindness, all those who uphold the vidya mantras and those who wish to accomplish the same—in short, all my noble sons and daughters who embrace the Mahayana—all perceive that eating meat brings obstacles to liberation. And since they wish to benefit themselves and others, they do not eat meat of any kind.

"The consciousness of beings focuses upon their physical form; a powerful clinging to this form takes hold and living beings thus identify their bodies as themselves. This is why a Bodhisattva, practicing compassion, should abstain from meat.

"O Mahamati, in order to avoid such things, a Bodhisattva—one who has compassion—should never eat meat of any kind. O Mahamati, Bodhisattvas keep themselves from meat of every kind. For those who feed on meat, already in this present life, their breath is foul and rank; they sleep with little ease, and they awake in pain. Dreadful visions haunt their dreams enough to make their hair stand up. Alone in solitude or else in empty houses, they fall victim to spirits that come and prey upon their vital strength. They easily succumb to fits of rage and the sudden onset of intense anxiety and dread. They lose all mastery of the way they eat and gorge themselves excessively. Food and drink and every vital nourishment they cannot properly digest. Worms infest their bowels, and they fall victim to contagious ailments, leprosy, and other ills. Yet, thus beset, they never think that eating meat might be the cause.

"I have declared that food can be either as wholesome as medicine or as dreadful as the flesh of children eaten and consumed as food. Meat is the food of ordinary people, Mahamati, but the Aryas reject it utterly. Meat consumption is the source of many evils; it is wholly destitute of virtue. It is not the food on which the wise sustain themselves. How could I permit my followers to taste of such unwholesome and unfitting nourishment as meat and blood? I say rather, Mahamati, that those who follow me should eat the food that Aryas themselves consume and that the common folk reject—food that is productive of good qualities and is free of taint—the wholesome foodstuffs of the wise of old. For my disciples, I prescribe a fitting nourishment: rice and barley, wheat and peas, every kind of bean and lentil, butter, oil, honey, treacle, fruits and sugar cane. I do this, Mahamati, because the time will come when fools whose minds are busy with speculation will chatter about the Vinaya. And strong in their desire for meat due to habit, they will say that flesh is wholesome fare.

"All this I teach for all who follow in the footsteps of the Buddhas of the past, for those who act with virtue, who are faithful and untouched by doubt. These are the noble daughters and the noble sons of Shakyamuni's lineage, who have no clinging to their bodies, lives, possessions, and to their sense of taste. Indeed they crave no tastes of any kind; they are compassionate and, like me, hold all beings in their love. They are great beings, Bodhisattvas. All living things are dear to them as though they were their own beloved children. May they keep this teaching in their minds!

"Once upon a time, O Mahamati, there was a king whose name was Senge Bangzang. He was a meat devourer. Indeed, if truth be told, he craved the taste of meats that are forbidden and at length began to eat the flesh of human beings. His family, his court, his relatives and friends all fled from him, as did all the people of his town and country. Thus abandoned, he suffered greatly. O Mahamati, even Indra, when in the past he came to be the ruler of the gods, due to his ingrained propensity for the consumption of meat, would at times take the shape of a hawk and do many cruel and evil things, even tearing at the breast of the innocent Shiden, the compassionate king, causing him great pain. Mahamati, the habit of eating meat, acquired over many lives, is the cause of many defects in oneself and is the source of the evils that one does to others—though one be born as Indra, let alone some lesser being.

"Mahamati, there is another tale about a ruler of men who was carried away by a powerful and unruly horse so that he lost his way and wandered in the wilderness. In order to survive, he took to living with a lioness, and children were at length born to them. The king's offspring, Kangtra and his brothers, growing up among the lions, became meat eaters. Owing to the habit acquired at this time, Kangtra continued to eat meat in his later lives even when he eventually became a king of men. And, Mahamati, this same king Kangtra and his brothers, even in their present existence, in the city of Khyimdun, still retain their craving for meat and even feed on flesh that is forbidden, wherefore they will be born as evil, flesh-devouring ghouls, both male and female. In times to come, Mahamati, in their subsequent existences, due to the longing for the taste of meat, they will be born as carnivorous beasts—lions, tigers, leopards, wolves, cats, foxes, and owls—and as *rakshasas* and other demons, all of them cruel devourers of flesh. And after such experience it will be hard for them ever to regain a human form, let alone attain nirvana. Such, Mahamati, are the defects of eating meat, and such indeed is the destiny of those who consume it in great quantity. On the other hand, to give up eating meat is the source of many excellent qualities. But, Mahamati, ordinary people know nothing of this, and therefore I have taught that Bodhisattvas should not eat meat, that they might understand.

"If people were to refrain from eating meat, Mahamati, animals would not be slain. For the majority of innocent beasts are slaughtered for the sake of money; few are killed for other reasons. Craving for the taste of meat can be unbearably strong and can lead even to the eating of human flesh, to say nothing of the flesh of beast and bird, wild or tame. Mahamati, people lusting for the taste of meat lay traps and nets to catch their prey. With such devices, hunters, butchers, fishermen, and their like take the lives of innocent creatures dwelling on the earth or in the air and water. Cruel folk such as these, devoid of pity like demonic rakshasas, who kill animals and devour them—such people will never generate compassion.

"Mahamati, every kind of meat, whether that which I have allowed the Shravakas, who are close to me, to consume, or that which I have not allowed, and all meat that is said to be unexamined,[4] is pernicious. In times to come, however, foolish people, ordained in my tradition, upholding the victory banner of the saffron robes, and claiming to be the children of Shakyamuni, will have their minds perverted by wrong thoughts. They will lose themselves in speculation about the rules of the Vinaya. Their ego clinging will be strong, and they will have a powerful craving for the taste of meat. They will concoct all sorts of excuses for eating meat, and thus they will blacken my reputation. They will examine the histories of events in the past and say, 'Since the Lord permitted meat to be eaten then, this shows that it is fitting nourishment.' They will say that the Lord taught that meat was healthy food, and they will go so far as to say that he himself enjoyed its taste. But, Mahamati, in none of my discourses did I ever give such general leave, and never did I teach that it was right to consider meat as wholesome fare.

"O Mahamati, you may believe that I have permitted the eating of meat; you may believe that Shravakas can eat it. But I say to you that I forbid it for the yogis dwelling in the charnel grounds who meditate on love. I forbid it for my noble sons and daughters who have embarked upon the true path of the Mahayana and who consider all beings as their own dear children. Mahamati, I do indeed forbid the eating of meat to all who consider living beings as their only children— the sons and daughters of my lineage who have faith in Dharma and are engaged in any of the paths of practice, yogis living in charnel grounds and practitioners meditating in solitude. The precepts of my Doctrine were formulated gradually, and they are successive steps upon a single path. Accordingly, the eating of meat is proscribed in the precepts of the Mahayana. Even though the flesh of beasts that have perished from ten natural causes is not forbidden to the Shravakas, nevertheless, in the Mahayana, all meat is utterly prohibited under all circumstances. And therefore, Mahamati, I have not given permission to anyone to consume meat.[5] I do not grant permission and I never shall. To all who wear the robe, O Mahamati, I declare that meat is an unfitting source of nourishment. Foolish people, benighted by their karma, who blacken my reputation by saying that even the Tathagata has eaten meat, will suffer long and meaninglessly, devoid of every joy. Moreover, Mahamati, my noble Shravakas in fact do not eat even ordinary food; how much less could they feed on the baneful fare of flesh and blood? O Mahamati, the Shravakas, Pratyekabuddhas, and Bodhisattvas eat the food of Dharma, which is by no means something material. Is there any need to speak of the food of Tathagatas? Mahamati, the Tathagatas are the *dharmakaya*; they are sustained by the food of Dharma. Their bodies are not formed of gross and solid matter; they are not sustained by material food. They have discarded all propensities related to samsara, the thirst for existence and the things of this life. They are utterly emancipated from all unwholesome and defiled tendencies; their minds are wholly freed in wisdom. They know everything; they see everything. They are replete with great compassion, loving all beings as though they were their only children. Therefore, O Mahamati, since I consider all beings as my children, how could I permit the Shravakas to eat my children's flesh? And how could I partake of it? It is wrong to say that I allowed the Shravakas to eat meat and that I myself have eaten it. For so it is:

> *The Bodhisattvas, mighty beings,*
> *Consume no alcohol; they eat*
> *No meat, no garlic, and no onion.*
> *This the Conquerors, the leaders of the flock, have taught.*
> *But common folk partake of evil-smelling fare;*
> *Their actions are unfitting.*

> *For flesh is food for wild and ravening beasts.*
> *It is unfitting food, the Buddha taught.*
> *The defects that arise from eating meat,*
> *The qualities that come when one abstains,*
> *However it may be for those who thus consume,*
> *All this, O Mahamati, you should understand.*

All flesh, of animals as well as of one's friends,
Derives from unclean substances, both blood and sperm;
And those who feed on flesh become a source of fear.
Therefore yogis shall refrain from eating meat.
Every kind of flesh, all onions and garlic,
Alcoholic drinks in various forms,
Leeks, wild garlic also——these indeed
Are foods the yogis shall reject.
All massaging with oil they spurn;
And since it is upon a bed
That living beings enter in the womb of pain,
On such the yogis do not sleep or take their rest.

From all such food derives the pride of self,
And from this pride all thoughts, and thence
Desire and craving, rise in all their strength.
All such foods therefore you should refuse.
Indeed it is from thought that craving comes;
By craving, then, the mind is rendered dull.
This dullness thence disturbs the body's elements;
Disease occurs with every movement crippled.

For sake of profit, animals are killed,
And wealth is given in exchange for meat.
Slayer, buyer, both are caught in sin,
And both will boil in hells of lamentation.
All those who contravene the Buddha's word,
Who with an evil attitude partake of meat,
Destroy their lives, both now and those to come,
And blight the discipline of Shakyamuni.

Such people, evil in their deeds, desire
What brings an endlessly enduring hell;
The destiny of those who feed on meat
Lies in the house of dreadful lamentation.
There is no meat that's pure in the three ways, [6]
And so you must refrain from eating flesh.

Those who are true yogis eat no meat:
This is the instruction of myself and all the Buddhas.
Creatures that devour each other
Are born again as carnivores and evil-smelling beasts.
Insane or universally despised,
They will be born among the outcasts:
Butchers, dyers, prostitutes, the lowest ranks,
Or else as flesh-devouring beasts and ghosts.
And after this, their present human life,
They will return as cats or evil wraiths.

And so in all my teachings I decry the eating of all flesh:
The Parinirvana *and* Angulimala,
The Lankavatara, Hastikakshya, *and* Mahamegha *sutras.* [7]
Therefore the Buddhas and the Bodhisattvas both,
And Shravakas as well have also criticized
The shameless eating of the flesh of beings.
It leads, in all one's later lives, to madness.

But if instead you fast from meat and other evil fare,
You will take birth in pure and human form,
As yogis, or as people rich in wisdom and in wealth.
The meat of beasts that you have seen or heard
Or think are killed for food, I utterly denounce.

Those born in families where meat is eaten
Know none of this, despite their cleverness.
Just as craving is an obstacle to freedom,
Even so are alcohol and meat.
People who eat meat in future times
Will ignorantly say that Buddha has declared
That eating meat is sinless and appropriate.
But yogis, moderate in what they eat,
Regarding food as nothing more than medicine,
Should not consume the flesh of beings, who are like
    their children.

Those who keep the company
Of tigers, lions, and the crafty fox
I censure—I who dwell in love.
To eat meat is to contravene
The Dharma, path to liberation.
Those who practice Dharma should refrain from meat,
For eating it they are a source of fear to beings.
To fast from meat—this is the banner of the Noble
    Beings' victory.

This concludes the sixth chapter of the *Lankavatara-sutra*, the quintessential teachings of the Buddhas, which treats of the question of meat eating.

The following passage is taken from the *Mahaparinirvana-sutra*:

THEN THE BODHISATTVA KASHYAPA addressed the Blessed Lord and said, "Lord, you do not partake of meat, and to eat meat is indeed unfitting. And if anyone were to ask me why this is so, I would answer that those who refrain from eating it are possessed of eight excellent qualities."

"That is very good," the Buddha answered Kashyapa. "You well perceive the intention of my mind. This indeed is how the Bodhisattvas, custodians of my Doctrine, should understand. Son of my lineage, even the Shravakas, those who keep close company with me, must not eat meat. Even if, in a gesture of faith, almsgivers provide them with meat, they must shrink from it as they would shrink from the flesh of their own children."

Then the Bodhisattva Kashyapa asked the Buddha, "But why indeed, O Lord and Tathagata, do you forbid the consumption of meat?"

"Son of my lineage!" the Lord replied. "Eating meat destroys the attitude of great compassion."

"But in the past, O Lord," asked Kashyapa, "did you not allow the eating of meat found suitable after it has been examined in three ways?"

"Yes," the Buddha said. "I allowed the eating of meat found suitable after threefold examination, in order to assist those who were striving to overcome their habit of eating meat."

"Why then," asked Kashyapa, "did you proscribe the eating of ten kinds of unexamined meat and so on, up to the nine types of examined meat?"

"This too I did," the Buddha said, "in order to help my followers in the overcoming of their habit. In short, all such provisions I made for one purpose: that the consumption of meat be brought to an end."

"But why," asked Kashyapa, "has the Tathagata allowed the flesh of fish as wholesome food?"

"Son of my lineage!" the Buddha answered. "I have never done so! I have described as healthy all sorts of food: sugar cane, rice, molasses, rye, barley, and so forth; milk, curd, butter, oil, and so on. I have likewise permitted my followers to wear robes of many kinds. But though I have so allowed them, such robes must be of the proper color! How much less could I allow the eating of fish simply to satisfy the desires of those who wish to eat it!"

"If you had allowed the eating of fish," said Kashyapa, "it would not make sense for you to advocate the five tastes, or milk, yogurt, buttermilk, butter, ghee, sesame oil, and so forth. It would be logical for you to forbid them, just as you have forbidden the keeping of ornaments, leather shoes, and gold and silver vessels."[8]

The Buddha said, "Son of my lineage, my teaching is not like that of the naked ascetics. I, the Tathagata, established rules of discipline in relation to specific individuals. Consequently, with a certain purpose in mind, I did give permission to eat meat regarded as suitable for consumption after it has been subjected to threefold examination. In other contexts, I have proscribed ten kinds of meat. And yet again, with someone else in mind, I have declared that it is improper to consume meat of any kind, even of animals that have died of natural causes. But I have affirmed, O Kashyapa, that henceforth, all those who are close to me should abstain from meat. For whether they are walking, sitting, standing, lying, or even sleeping, meat eaters are a source of terror to animals who can smell them—just as everyone is frightened at the smell of a lion. My son! People who dislike the smell of garlic turn away from those who eat it. What need is there to mention the disadvantages of such food? It is the same with meat eaters.

When animals smell meat, they are terrified; they are afraid of being killed. Any animal, in field or stream or flying in the sky, flees, believing that the person in question is their very enemy. This is why I do not allow the Bodhisattvas to eat meat. It is true that they may put on a show of eating meat as a means of bringing beings to liberation. But even though they appear to be meat eaters, they are not. Son of my lineage! Bodhisattvas refrain even from eating pure food; how much more do they abstain from meat!

"My son! It will happen that after I have passed into nirvana, and after the Aryas (even those endowed with limitless life span, accomplished through the four noble paths)[9] have gone beyond sorrow, the sacred Dharma will decline. All that will remain of it will be but a pale shadow. The monks will only make a pretense of observing the discipline, and their reading and recitation of the sutras will indeed be meager. They will crave food to sustain their physical bodies; they will dress themselves in black and evil raiment. They will be utterly devoid of noble bearing. They will care for livestock, cattle, and sheep. They will be carriers of wood and hay. They will have long hair and nails. All this will come to pass. They may don the saffron robe, but they will be no different from hunters. They may have a gentle bearing and may go with downcast eyes, but they will be more like cats stalking mice. They will claim again and again that they have brought their emotions into subjection, but all the while they will be plagued by pain and sickness, by drowsiness and impurity. Hypocrites, they will adopt the outward habits of religion, but inwardly they will be in the grip of anger, jealousy, and desire—no different from those who follow false religions. They will not be virtuous; their piety will be a mere pretense.

They will entertain wrong views and criticize the authentic Dharma. People such as this will mar the principles of discipline laid down by the Tathagata: the teachings of the Vinaya, the teachings of the path and fruit of perfect freedom. They will sully my teachings on the avoidance of carelessness. They will even pervert the extremely profound doctrines and concoct sutras and rules of discipline of their own invention. They will say and write that the Tathagata has given them permission to eat meat, and that such is the word of Buddha. They will fight among themselves, each claiming to be the child of virtuous Shakyamuni.

"O my son! That will be the time when monks will become hoarders of grain and eaters of fish. They will have dainty dishes for their butter and parasols of precious stuff, and they will put on shoes of leather. The teachings that they give to kings, ministers, and common householders will be nothing but the science of omens, astrology, fortune-telling, and the care of the body. They will keep servants, man and maid, and they will use gold and silver, precious stones, sapphires, crystals, pearls, and corals; they will wear necklaces and will enjoy all sorts of fruit. They will play sports and amuse themselves with painting and sculpture. They will teach literature; they will plow their fields and harvest their crops. They will cast spells; they will prepare drugs and heal with words of power. They will teach music, dancing, and singing and all sorts of handicrafts like the preparation of incense and flower garlands and basket weaving. But you should understand that only those who forsake such unprofitable activities are truly close to me."

"Lord," said Kashyapa, "monks, nuns, and lay practitioners all depend on benefactors. When they go for alms and receive food containing meat, what should they do? How should they examine it?"

"They should separate," the Buddha replied, "the meat from the rest of the food, which should then be washed and then consumed. If it happens that their bowl has been stained by the meat but is not defiled by the evil smell or taste, there is no fault in eating from it. But if someone gives them quantities of meat, let them not accept it. If meat is mingled with their food, let them not eat of it, else they will be at fault. If I were to explain in detail the prohibition of meat and all its rules, there would be no end! But it is now time for me to pass beyond suffering; therefore I have explained it to you only in part."

The above was taken from the section of the *Mahaparinirvana-sutra* called *The Answering of Questions*.

The following passage is taken from the *Angulimala-sutra*:

MANJUSHRI DECLARED, "It is because of the tathagatagarbha that the Buddhas refrain from eating meat." And the Lord added:

"So it is, Manjushri. There is not a single being, wandering in the chain of lives in endless and beginningless samsara, that has not been your mother or your sister. An individual, born as a dog, may afterward become your father. Each and every being is like an actor playing on the stage of life. One's own flesh and the flesh of others is the same flesh. Therefore the Enlightened Ones eat no meat. Moreover, Manjushri, the *dharmadhatu* is the common nature of all beings, therefore Buddhas refrain from eating meat."

Manjushri also said, "There are, Lord, other, quite ordinary beings who also abstain from meat."

"Whatever worldly people do," the Lord replied, "that is in harmony with the Buddha's word should be considered as the teachings of the Buddha himself."

It is said in the *Sutra of Close Mindfulness:*[10]

IF, WITH THE WISDOM THAT ACCRUES from hearing the teachings, a monk understands the fully ripened effects of actions, and if he contemplates the world of *pretas*, or famished spirits, he will perceive the condition of such beings who subsist on blood. And if the monk reflects with wisdom about the actions that cause such beings to be so reborn, he will see that pretas are beings who, in their past lives, drank blood for their pleasure and in order to increase their strength. They were, likewise, sunk in cruelty, anger, jealousy, and avarice. They deceived their families, and, craving blood, they killed. After death, such people fell into the lower realms and have been born as blood-drinking spirits. By the power of their karma, they are born as spirits in the very places they frequented in their earlier existences. Here the inhabitants call them demons and make offerings to them, circumambulating their dwelling places and making blood sacrifices. Such blood-drinking spirits, intoxicated with human gore, are harmful to the population. And it is then said that they are powerful and able to work great miracles. As for their life span, as long as they do not abandon their evil actions and their karmic impetus is not exhausted, they live as powerful pretas. Even when they are released from this condition, their behavior will follow the same pattern, owing to the effects of their karma, and thus they will wander in samsara. If, once out of a hundred lifetimes, they have the chance to be reborn as a man or a woman, it may be observed that they become worldly *daka*s or *dakini*s.

If, with the wisdom that accrues from hearing the teachings, a monk understands the fully ripened effects of actions, and if he contemplates the world of famished spirits, he will understand the condition of such beings who subsist on flesh. And if the monk reflects with wisdom on the actions that bring about such a birth, he will observe that these pretas are beings who in their previous lives were involved, out of greed, in the sale of meat—the flesh of cows, horses, game, pigs, or sheep—and that they acted with great dishonesty and fraudulently sold it at a high price. When they died, such beings fell into the lower realms and were born as flesh-devouring pretas. They become wild and ferocious spirits, haunting crossroads and marketplaces, streets, roads and wastelands, villages or temples. Existence as a powerful preta with miraculous powers is not the exclusive outcome of evil and atrocious negativity; the positive action of giving (such small items as plants and vegetables) also plays a part. This indeed is what accounts for their possessing miraculous powers. The common people appease such spirits by means of animal sacrifices: offerings of buffalos, wild animals, snakes, sheep, and other beasts. And as long as such spirits, being evil, do not abandon their dreadful behavior and jealous anger, and as long as their karmic impetus is not exhausted, they will continue to take birth in that state. Later on, when they are released from it, they will still exhibit the same patterns of behavior and will wander in samsara in conditions that are in keeping with their actions.

And if, once out of a hundred lifetimes—thanks to some positive act—they have the fortune to achieve a human birth (as rare as a blind turtle coming to the surface of the ocean to find its head inside a yoke floating at random on the sea), they will become meat eaters, they will become butchers who cut up the carcasses of animals, and they will work in slaughterhouses.

It is said also in the same sutra:

THOSE WHOSE ACTIONS are evil are the ones who will fill the Hell of Great Heat, experiencing therein the fruits of their wickedness. It is there that they will boil for hundreds of thousands of years because of their willful harm. Their own evil actions have thus become their enemies. When they gain release, they will flee, searching for a protector, a refuge, or help. But in the distance they will see packs of ravenous hounds, with jaws agape and teeth like sharpened diamonds, which race toward them and encircle them with their terrible baying. The denizens of hell will try to escape, but the hounds of hell will overtake and devour them whole: sinews and flesh, joint and bone, leaving nothing, not even a fragment the size of a mustard seed! Body and limbs will be completely eaten up. And this experience of being devoured by dogs will occur again and again. All this is said to be the result of killing living beings for the sake of enjoying their meat.

The following is taken from the tantra of *The Compassionate One, Churning the Depths of Samsara*:[11]

IF ONE EATS MEAT, actions motivated by hatred are performed. Therefore meat eating constitutes a grave cause [of such wrongdoing]. Actions motivated by stupidity are performed if one drinks blood, which therefore is a serious secondary cause. A greater defilement comes from eating even a small fragment of meat than from drinking alcohol. It is a greater evil to drink one drop of the blood of an animal killed by oneself than to eat for a hundred years the flesh of animals killed by others. This is due to the karmic principle of cause and effect. Beings of the three worlds are alarmed at the sight of what they call blood. And when they see it being drunk, beings in the three dimensions of existence faint away. Every kind of karmic obscuration is produced thereby.

As for alcohol, if one drinks but does not, while drunk, commit negative deeds, one will accumulate (the causes of) a single birth among the pretas. But if one commits an evil action, one will be born in the hot hells. If one eats the flesh of animals that one has not oneself killed, the result is to experience a single life (lasting one *kalpa*) in hell. If one eats the meat of beasts that one has killed or one has caused another to kill, one must spend a hundred thousand kalpas in hell. If one partakes of the blood of an animal killed by another, the effect will be likewise proportionate to the cause. Consequently, if one consumes a quantity of blood corresponding to a jug of ale sufficient for twenty people, one will be born in places where one will not even hear the name of the Three Jewels for a kalpa. And if one drinks blood throughout one's life, one will wander for countless aeons in samsara. To drink the blood of living animals leads to seven incarnations in the condition of an animal. If one drinks only once the blood of an animal that one has oneself killed, one will be born in a hell where one will be forced to drink molten bronze. If one were to eat the flesh and blood, still warm, of animals that one has oneself slaughtered, in a quantity equal to one's own body weight, one will be born in one's very next life in a hell of molten boiling bronze and will have to stay there for a kalpa. If one eats meat red and raw and drinks raw blood, after seven lifetimes one will be born in hells where molten bronze will be poured into one's mouth. If one eats meat and blood that have been cooked, one will be born ten lifetimes later in the hell of molten boiling bronze. Meat and blood, therefore, are foods that bring down ruin on the three worlds.

The consumption of meat that has been handled and passed on by many owners brings with it a less grievous fault. For example, if one eats meat that has passed through the hands of a hundred people, one will suffer birth in hell only after a hundred lifetimes. Similarly, the eating of meat that has been handled by ten people will bring an infernal existence after ten lifetimes, and so on proportionately.

In the same way, it is more serious to eat the flesh of an animal that has been killed than to eat the flesh of an animal that has died from natural causes. It is a hundred times more serious to eat even once the flesh of an animal that one has oneself killed than it is to eat the flesh of an animal killed by others. And it is ten times worse to eat the flesh of an animal that has been killed at one's own request than to eat the meat of a beast one has killed oneself. One should understand how this scale of values is to be applied. It is also said that if one continually consumes meat, blood, and alcohol, which nurture the three poisons, the five defiled emotions will manifest.

It is written in the tantra *Embodiment of Wisdom*[12] as follows:

MEAT AND BLOOD are very negative foods and give off a strong smell. Spirits that feed on odors will come and steal away the vital energy and physical essences of those who consume meat, causing them to lose their healthy radiance. . . . If one craves the five great substances, such as meat and blood, looking on them as truly existent things, one will eventually become a spirit that lives upon the smell of blood.

Similarly it is written in the tantra *Embodiment of Awareness:*[13]

> *When beings feed on flesh and gore,*
> *Dreadful and foul-reeking food,*
> *Evil wraiths that live on smells,*
> *Sniffing out the stench of blood,*
> *Will steal away their vital strength*
> *And rob them of their radiance and their health.*
> *Why do these people thus indulge themselves?*

IF INDEED ONE CRAVES the five great substances, for example, blood, considering them as truly existent, one will be reborn as a dangerous spirit that lives on the stench of blood and takes the terrifying form of one of the seven mothers. Anyone who drifts into such a dependency will wander in the land of Lanka in the form of a dreadful, flesh-devouring demoness.

According to a text belonging to the Kriya tantra, the *Amogha Pasha:*[14]

ALCOHOL, MEAT, GARLIC, wild garlic, leek—alone or mixed with other food—should be especially shunned.

Another text[15] belonging to the same tantra states:

THOSE WHO WISH to keep the precepts must abstain completely from alcohol, meat, onion, leeks, and the remnants of the offerings to the gods.

In the tantra of Akshobya[16] it is written that:

CURD, MILK, BUTTER, sweet substances, sweet fried pancakes, bread, and rice should be consumed in moderation. All evil-smelling foods should be rejected, such as meat, alcohol, garlic, and so forth.

The Lotus Net, the root tantra of Lord Avalokita,[17] says:

STALE OFFERINGS, garlic, soiled or discarded food, meat and food from the hands of butchers, and water containing insects—all these should be rejected.

The Compendium of the Mahayana[18] by the Acharya Krishnapa says:

ONE SHOULD ALWAYS ABSTAIN from meat, fish, alcohol, garlic, radish; and one should likewise refrain from dyeing cloth,[19] pressing sesame seeds, farming, and so forth.

In *The Compendium of Views*,[20] the teacher renowned as Jamy-ang Mi'i Wangpo says:

TEACHERS AND HOUSEHOLDERS, religious people and ascetics who eat meat and drink alcohol will become pretas when they die. . . . Parents should not give their children meat and fish to eat nor alcohol to drink. Children should be fed on milk and butter, for example, but not meat.

In his *Stages of Meditation*,[21] Kamalashila says:

WHEN YOGIS MEDITATE, they should always refrain from eating meat, fish, and so forth. For such foods are at variance with their meditation. They should be moderate in their eating habits.

In his *Thought-Free Meditation*,[22] Vimalamitra says:

AT ALL TIMES, yogis should avoid eating meat and fish. They should eat in proper measure and partake of food that is in harmony with the teachings.

Gyalse Thogme also says:

> *When beings die a natural death*
> *Who have, from time without beginning, been our close-loved*
>   *kin,*
> *We weep. This shows indeed how wrong it is*
> *To eat the flesh of beasts that have been killed for meat.*

Likewise the root tantra of *Kalachakra* says:

> *Wicked people, hard to train,*
> *Kill harmless beasts*
> *As sacrifice to gods and for their ancestors,*
> *To gain protection, profit, and fulfill their aims.*
> *To buy the meat, to wish to eat it, is indeed an evil act.*

This passage shows that if one wishes to eat meat and buys what one knows has come from animals that have been slaughtered for commercial purposes, one commits a negative action.

The commentary on the *Kalachakra-tantra*[23] says:

ONE SHOULD NOT BUY MEAT, nor should one offer animals in sacrifice to the gods and ancestral spirits. For the Buddha never allowed "marked meat" to be eaten. And by "marked meat" he meant the flesh of animals that have been killed and purchased for food, as well as animals marked for sacrifice.

Most especially, no one should eat the flesh of human beings. The *Vinaya-sutra* specifies that "human flesh should not be consumed under any circumstances." The extensive commentary on this text[24] goes even further and specifies that "if one eats human flesh for medicinal purposes or for any other reason, one commits an infraction." If one eats the red, raw meat (of animals), without this being necessary for the curing of an illness, one commits an infraction. The *Vinaya-sutra* says that "the consumption of raw meat for nonmedical reasons constitutes an infraction," and to this the extensive commentary adds that "if one eats raw flesh as part of the practice of the Mantrayana and so on (without its being needed for medicinal purposes), one commits an infraction associated with the residual fault[25] of provoking disputes in the sangha. Furthermore, it creates a cause for being reborn as an evil spirit." Again the *Vinaya-sutra* says, "One must not eat the meat of a tiger, nor the flesh of elephants, horses, and snakes. One must not eat the meat of animals with undivided hooves, nor of foxes, monkeys, woodpeckers, crows, vultures, water birds, dogs, cats, hawks, owls and other carrion birds, gray ducks, bats, snow lizards, apes, and insects."

Commenting on the *Lankavatara-sutra*, the abbot Jnanavajra wrote as follows:

THE ENTIRE RANGE of the Buddha's teachings, starting from the first turning of the wheel of Dharma, with the exposition of the Four Noble Truths, up to and including the teachings of the Vidyadhara-pitaka,[26] are covered by Pratimoksha, Bodhisattva, and Vidyadhara vows and precepts. The precepts connected with the consumption of food constitute three gradual steps in a single path. For this reason, even the meat qualified by threefold purity, which the Shravakas are permitted to eat, is proscribed for practitioners of the higher vehicles. The reason for this is to prevent the higher and very important precepts from being impaired. The flesh of animals that have died by any of the ten natural kinds of death is not denied to the Shravakas. But in the higher vehicles, in order to draw carnivorous spirits onto the path, and so that practitioners do no harm, whether directly or indirectly, to living beings, every kind of meat is strictly forbidden, at all times and under all circumstances. There are no special conditions under which it may be eaten. . . . One should eat in moderation even the food of sages, which is like medicine. One should always refrain from meat, in the knowledge that it is unwholesome food.

Another commentator on the *Lankavatara-sutra*, the Acharya Jnanashribhadra, has written as follows:

THE OMNISCIENT ONE has declared that to eat meat and to encourage others to eat meat is an evil act because it causes harm to beings. The Buddha forbade the consumption of all meat that is not pure in the three ways, but he did not consider it wrong to partake of meat that is so. Meat that is completely pure in the three ways is the flesh of animals that one has not killed, that one has not ordered to be killed, and that one has not seen to be killed. If without evil intentions and expectancy one donates such meat to someone, just as if one were giving them rice to eat, it is quite pure and as beneficial as medicine. But even this kind of meat is forbidden to Bodhisattvas, who practice compassion. Most especially it is forbidden to the practitioners of the Mantrayana. For they are bound to respect beings and consider them indeed as *yidam* deities. Only when one rids oneself of every craving for the taste of sense objects is liberation gained.

Prince Firm-in-Faith is recorded as saying:[27]

LISTEN TO ME, O king of flesh-devouring demons. All who kill animals and feed on their flesh will have their lives cut short, and most of them will go to hell. Others will slay and devour them in retaliation. For the karmic effect is similar to its cause. Listen to me, O king of flesh-devouring demons. Many there are who are brought to ruin by the evil company they keep. If you eat the meat and blood of beings who have been your parents, you will go to hell.

And the great Lord Atisha has said:

INWARDLY, SWEEP AWAY the impurities of the five poisons. Outwardly, sweep away all foul dirt and filth. And between these two, sweep away the intervening impurity of laziness and indifference. Sweep away bad food: meat, garlic, onions, and alcohol. Rid yourself of all nourishment that is unclean and inappropriate. Those of you who live on alms and follow a specific time schedule for meals, sweep away the impurity of eating at improper times.

Once in times gone by, the Kadampa lama Zhangtön Darma Gyaltsen and Changchub Zangpo met some tea merchants on the road to Dam. They begged for alms. One of the merchants, a Khampa, offered them some dried meat, the flanks and hind legs of an animal. "Alas!" cried Changchub Zangpo, "this is the lower part of my mother's corpse. How long it has been kept for me! How can I, her child, eat her flesh? If we who wear the robes of Buddha's disciples eat our mothers' flesh, we have indeed turned into jackals!" He began to recite the mantra *Om Kamkani Kamkani*[28] and sat there with a brooding countenance. The rough Khampa was afraid; he made one hasty prostration to him and ran off, taking his meat with him.

Zhangtön smiled at Changchub Zangpo and said, "You had parents who had faith in the Dharma, and long ago you turned away from village life and took vows from a good lama. Later on, you studied well, and your feelings of sadness on seeing the flesh of an animal, once your parent, is indeed a great wonder. Only now that I am full of years and have lived long in this world do I see such a thing!"

When another old Khampa asked him which tradition he belonged to, Zhangtön lama replied that he was a Kadampa monk.

"I take refuge in the Kadampas!" exclaimed the old Khampa. "I hope that a large Kadampa monastery will be founded also in Kham!"

It is written in the *Sutra Describing Karmic Cause and Effect:*[29]

IF YOU EAT MEAT and chew on bones, you will lose your teeth! If you eat intestines and the meat of dogs and swine, you will be reborn in an infernal state that is filled with filth. If you eat fish after scraping off their scales, you will be born in the hell of sword-forests.

And the precious teacher Dromtön declared:

YOU PRACTITIONERS WHO selflessly give up your own flesh and blood but who nevertheless eat the flesh of your parents and drink their blood, how you will lament when you are pursued again and again and forced to pay for their lives with your own!

Once, in the past, there was a good and compassionate Indian master who visited Tibet. Having observantly taken note of everything, he remarked, "I notice that whatever the Tibetan practitioners undertake is excellent. Nevertheless all of them eat meat; they do not abstain from it, and this is not good."

The great lama Jamyang Gyamtso said:

ALL PHENOMENA ARISE in interdependence. Owing to the causal link that exists between the meat eaters and the animal killers, the meat eaters themselves constitute a cause and pretext for the evil act of killing. As a consequence, the karmic result of slaughtering a cow, for instance, will ripen on both the meat eater and the animal killer. The only difference consists in the extent of the effects. This is an inescapable fact. The reason for this, the Kadampas say, is that those who eat meat are perpetrating an act that is similar to killing. As a result of this, the consumption of meat is proscribed in both the Hinayana and the Mahayana. Therefore, let all practitioners abandon meat eating as much as they can.

In *The Precious Heap*[30] it is specified as follows:

THE PERMISSION to eat meat and fish is a teaching that is to be interpreted. For the Buddha declared that if he had forbidden meat from the very start, there were some who would never have entered the teachings. It is with skill, therefore, that he only gradually excluded it. On the other hand, as an antidote for those who claim that the mere abstention from meat is their great and all-sufficient practice, the Buddha declared the contrary by saying that meat eating does not constitute a hindrance on the path. He said this to put down those who considered that they were superior on account of being vegetarians. The fact is, however, that the consumption of meat is proscribed in both the Hinayana and Mahayana. It is equally banned for the simple reason that it entails an action that is akin to killing. In particular, the Buddha decreed that Bodhisattvas should abstain from all meat.

Once, long ago, the noble Katyayana contracted smallpox and was told by his doctor that he should consume goat's meat and goat's blood and that he should apply them to his skin. But the former answered that he would die rather than transgress the precepts. He did not eat the meat and so passed beyond suffering.

When the lord Taklung Thangpa was on the point of death, he was requested to eat some soup with fat in it, as this would cure his disease. "Throughout my life," he replied, "I have been able to keep the precepts. Why should I break them now that I am on the point of death?" He ignored his doctor's advice and so passed away.

There are many stories like this. We are informed by many accounts of how Atisha, Drikung Kyobpa and his closest disciple, as well as Taklung Thangpa and many other great beings used molasses, honey, and so on, instead of meat, and how they used milk or curd instead of alcohol. And this was a matter of great rejoicing for Pönlop Lochen.[31] Gotsangpa Natsok Rangdrol said that he was wonderfully inspired by the practice of Atisha, Taklung Thangpa, and other great beings, especially when he saw how the majority of monks in his day prepared their ganachakra offering—using alcohol simply out of desire and consuming it in a very ordinary way.

The story goes that long ago, in the time of Buddha Dipamkara, there was born, in the town of Drucha, to an ugly man and his beautiful Brahmin wife, a son with red eyes and sharp canine teeth. Even when a baby, he would tear worms and flies apart and gobble them down. When he grew up, he used to kill wild beasts and fish whenever he could and would eat meat and drink wine completely without restraint. He eventually met his death, stabbed in the heart with a black poisoned dagger. He at once fell into an infernal realm where he was torn apart and eaten alive by wild, carnivorous animals, while his demon tormentors poured molten metal into his mouth. Amid his screams, he shouted, "Because in my past life I ate the flesh of animals, now wild beasts are devouring my flesh. Because I craved meat and blood, now others wish only to devour me. The meat seemed so delicious while I was eating it, but now that the fully ripened effect is upon me, how dreadful it is! Drinking wine has resulted in the guardians of hell pouring molten metal into my mouth. Because I drank without restraint, now others torment me without reprieve. The alcohol seemed so delicious when I drank it then, but now when I feel its fully ripened effects, what horror!" Afterward, he was reborn as a preta and suffered great torments yet again.

And then there was the king, Senge Bangzang, whose diet consisted exclusively of meat. In due course, his craving grew to such a pitch that he eventually consumed the flesh of a young child. His court and people fled from him. He therefore suffered intensely and, after his death, was reborn in the lower realms.

Once upon a time, when Prince Firm-in-Faith journeyed to the land of rakshasas and asked the demon sentinel why he did not devour him, he received the following answer. "Your teacher Shakyamuni," cried the rakshasa, "has granted us—

flesh-devouring demons that we are—the *upavasa* vow[32] to be observed every full moon. He has explained to us the many evil consequences of eating meat and has told us that the meat we eat is actually the flesh of our former fathers and mothers. He recommended that we renounce it. But since meat and blood are our natural fare, we cannot do without it all the time, and we therefore do so on the fifteenth day of the month. If any humans come here on that day, not only do we not harm them, but we actually help them!"

Again, it is told that King Chömé presented King Pawo with the meat of a deer and asked him whether he would eat it. The latter replied that he would not, for fresh red meat was not appropriate even for carnivorous spirits, let alone human beings. Finally, the story is told that once, when two yogis, practitioners of the sadhana of Hayagriva and Varahi, were on the point of accomplishment, they ate some pork and horse-meat. This created an obstacle to the accomplishment, which therefore did not manifest.

In *The Stainless Light,*[33] the great commentary on the *Kalachakra-tantra,* it is said that Lord Buddha predicted that the yogis of the Mantrayana would eat meat, but that meat itself is always the product of killing. If people did not slaughter them for meat, animals would remain unharmed. Without a meat eater, there is no animal killer. For this reason both consumer and slaughterer are both guilty of the act of killing. Furthermore, practitioners of the Secret Mantra must observe daily the fourth samaya (of the fourteen root samayas).[34] This was surely the Lord's instruction.

Venerable Milarepa said:

> *Harmless beasts you slay and eat;*
> *You make and taste a drink to make you drunk*

And lay the cause for the Reviving Hell.
Oh, do not jump into the gulf with open eyes.
Take care, you gods and humankind, take care!
When pricked by thorns, you cannot bear the pain,
And yet you kill and eat the flesh of living beings.
How harsh will be the prickles of Reviving Hell,
When skin will be flayed from your burning limbs!
So take away your dreadful blood-red meat.
Here it is, unspoiled and quite untouched;
Take it now and use it as you wish!

It is recounted in the short biography of Lord Phagmo Drupa that he cherished the three trainings and abstained entirely from all evil sustenance such as meat. He would not even eat soup seasoned with animal fat. Moreover, when he was poisoned and close to death, he was advised that if he were to drink a cup of beer that had been blessed with mantras he would be cured. But he would not take it and so risked his life.

The lama king Yeshe Ö once addressed a message to the Tibetan people, who, he considered, were practicing wrongly:

Small is your compassion, less than that of cannibals!
Great your love of meat, more keen than hawks and wolves!
Strong your lust, you're worse than bulls and donkeys!
You swarm around your drink far more than wasps and
  midges!
Your sense of dirt and cleanliness is less than dogs and pigs!
Before the deities you set your excrement,
Your urine, sperm, and blood—
Alas for you, you're destined for the bogs of rotting flesh!
You flout the teachings of the Tripitaka,

Alas for you, you will be born in hells of Torments
    Unsurpassed!
And beasts whom you should liberate you merely slay,
Alas for you, these deeds will ripen in the state of rakshasas!
Your lusting for the bliss of union—
Alas for you—will bring you birth as womb-infesting
    parasites!

The Omniscient Changkya once declared:

Before them on a dish to do them proud
Are piled the bones and bleeding meat of slaughtered beasts.
They wave their knives and suck their spit-flecked gleaming
    chops
You'd think they're off to fight a demon horde—
These seeming virtuous monks, oh, pity them!

Once, after many stories had been told about the evils of meat eating, Drukpa Kunleg said:

IT IS SAID THAT THE Buddha taught how wrong it is to eat fish, pigs, and garlic. To that I will add that in the general Mahayana, the Buddha forbids the eating of any kind of meat because it weakens compassion and because there is a danger that the consumption of meat is harmful to the lives of those who eat it and might even render them mentally defective. Specifically, however, it is said in all the sutras and tantras that all beings have been our parents. This is something one can feel and be convinced of—they have all been our parents from beginningless time. If we piled up the bones of all who have been our fathers, or gathered together the milk that all those who have been our mothers have lavished upon us, the triple world itself would not be big enough to contain it all.

And if people were really to think about it, *who* would be able to eat the flesh of their own parents and children?

People think that it is enough that the Shravakas have no desire for flesh and refrain from improper meat. And excusing themselves by appealing to texts such as: "If Shravakas refrain from meat that is permitted (namely, pure in the three ways) they are behaving like Devadatta," they eat meat. For example, you wouldn't say—would you?—that a woman who's been ignored by three sex maniacs is viable goods. So it's not all right—is it?—to eat meat that has been hawked (and rejected) in three markets?[35] If people casuistically stick to the literal sense and ignore the meaning of the teaching, they are wrong.

These are the words of Drukpa Kunleg himself. Moreover, once, when he was on his travels, he saw how in certain monasteries there were many monks who loved meat and who bought it greedily from the butchers. "This monastery," he said scornfully, "is a lair of wolves and so is that! It is said in the *Shiksasamuccaya* that one should preserve one's body with medicinal food. This does not include fish and meat, for these are forbidden in the *Lankavatara-sutra*, where the Buddha declared that compassionate Bodhisattvas should refrain from meat of any kind. The *Shiksasamuccaya* also says that when the Vinaya stipulates that meat that is pure in the three ways may be eaten and should not be rejected, it does so to demolish the feelings of superiority of those who think that in refraining from meat altogether they are holding to the purest view. It is also a skillful measure for the sake of those who, because of their craving for meat, would otherwise be unable to enter the teachings, even though they have the karmic fortune to do so. This is also stated in the *Lankavatara*, which says that the teachings and precepts were set forth in a gradual manner as steps of a single path. Thus, the permission to indulge in meat, granted at the Pratimoksha stage, is proscribed in the Mahayana, in which even the eating of the flesh of animals that have died from one of the ten kinds of natural death is totally outlawed."

With regard to the gradual formulation of the three precepts concerning meat eating, as propounded step by step by the Buddha, the teachers of the past say that in the Vinaya, the consumption of human flesh and the flesh of animals with undivided hooves is first of all proscribed.[36] Later on, meat is generally forbidden except for what is pure in the three ways. These two Vinaya precepts, followed by the general Mahayana precept that forbids Bodhisattvas to eat meat of any kind, including the flesh of animals that have died naturally, are the three precepts concerning meat.

Khyentse Rinpoche[37] said that in the scriptures he had only ever seen such injunctions as: "I have not allowed, I do not allow, and I will not allow the eating of meat. I have told all the ordained sangha that it is improper to eat meat. . . . From now on, the Shravakas should not eat meat." By contrast, he said that he had never come across the Buddha saying, "Mark the heads of yaks and sheep that are to be killed." Khyentse Rinpoche also said that the villagers in his neighborhood would kill large and fattened animals out of desire for their meat, and they would bring the liver and other pieces of meat as offering to the lamas and meditators.

"Alas, these people!" he cried. "How generous they are and what pure perception of the lamas they must have! How brave they are, being able to kill like that! They do not think that killing is a serious fault! They think that their little gift will do them a lot of good and cleanse away their sins; and they think that the lamas can liberate beings as easily as pulling them with iron chains. It's totally impossible! Nagarjuna has said in his *Letter to a Friend*:[38]

> *Were I to make a pill of mud just berry-sized*
> *For every mother who has given me birth,*
> *The earth itself indeed would not suffice.*

"All beings have been our mothers, but ordinary people do not recognize them as such, and that is why they are able to kill them. Of course, we Dharma people cannot eat meat, and why? Because our mothers and fathers, our brothers and sisters, our friends of the past who were so dear to us—here they are in front of us! They have become these bent and stupid creatures called animals, who do not know what is to be done and what is to be rejected. They may have horns on their heads, they may walk on four legs, but they are our parents and friends from the past. People never think about this. They imprison animals in pens and enclosures; it is quite terrible. And when these animals, all our parents, siblings, wives, and friends from the past, have fallen into the hands of their butchers, wicked, cruel men without the slightest trace of compassion, they tremble with fear, terrified beyond measure at the mere sight of their executioners. Their eyes fill with tears and they gasp with fright. They think to themselves, 'Who will help me now? There is nowhere for me to run; I cannot fly away; there is only death for me!' They are overwhelmed with dread, their suffering more terrible than if they were on the very brink of the fiery pits of hell. They are thrown on their backs on the ground, their eyes staring from their sockets. And rubbing his hands with satisfaction, the butcher slices open their bellies with his knife and without the slightest hesitation sends them onto the path of the next life. What is there here that could possibly be pleasing to the lama? With complete trust in Guru Rinpoche,[39] I beg you with tears in my eyes—all you who love me, do not kill even to save your own lives. For the Buddha has said in the *Sutra of Close Mindfulness*: 'Those who kill a single being will boil in the ephemeral hell for one intermediate kalpa.' The sutras say that to make presents of meat, alcohol, poison, and weapons is a negative action, whether directly or indirectly. Therefore it is quite improper to give meat as a gift. Even those who know no other practice should at least abstain from meat as much as they can. May these words of truth come to pass!"

The Vajradhara Reting Trichen said:

BODHISATTVAS WHO CRAVE the taste of meat weaken their compassion. They should abstain!

In Khedrup Je's commentary on *The Three Vows*, it is said that, on the whole, only the Bodhisattvas are required to abstain from meat. Therefore, all who have taken the vow of bodhichitta, whether they be monks, nuns, or lay people, must abstain from meat. For if Bodhisattvas, who have thus become an object of praise, eat meat, a strong desire for the taste of it will grow in them. As a result, their compassion will wane. Therefore the fully ordained, the shramaneras, kings, ministers, leaders, and lay people who practice the Mahayana should refrain from eating meat.

Khedrup Je predicted that even those who have taken the Bodhisattva vow, even those who have recited the formula of bodhichitta hundreds of times will not consider even the conscious killing of thousands of animals or the inducing of others to do the same as wrong; no need to talk about their abstinence from meat. He was so right, and we can see that in our own days his prophecy has come to pass!

Therefore we must regard the eating of meat as contrary to the teachings. We must get used to the idea that it is wrong to crave meat, and we must reject it! If we think to ourselves, "How good meat is for us. How clean and wholesome it is. How delicious it tastes!" the consequence will be that whenever meat and blood are placed before us—as if it were no more than rice and tsampa, milk and butter—we will feel an intense craving and we will be unable to resist. This is why Khedrup Je said that just as we are about to put it in our mouths, we should reflect that the meat is something filthy, that has arisen from sperm and blood. Furthermore, we should remember that the flesh has come from beings who have been, from beginningless time, our own mothers and our own children. And we should conclude that it is deeply wrong to crave their meat, just as it would be utterly terrible to long for the flesh of our own children!

We should ponder the dangers implicit in the desire for meat and reflect, in accordance with the teachings, that if we go hunting and fishing, we are turning into butchers and killers. If we buy meat, we are inciting others to kill animals for their flesh. If we sell the meat of slaughtered beasts for profit, if we long for meat, we are like Senge Bangzang and Prince Kangtra, who killed human beings and devoured their flesh. Smelling the revolting odor, animals will flee from us. It is said that the accomplishment of the vidya mantra and the development of great love and compassion will be impeded.

Therefore, in our desire for meat, we should never say that the Vinaya advocates the eating of meat. It is said that never, even in our dreams, should we say that meat eating is without fault. Experience proves that when people who aspire to enlightenment and cultivate bodhichitta eat meat, their compassion weakens and their determination with it. On the other hand, it is taught that when people keep themselves in check in order to curb their desire for the taste of meat, and when they abstain from meat of every kind, pure or impure in the three ways—both the meat of slaughtered animals and of animals that have died naturally—this is truly a great wonder!

Even non-Buddhists refrain from eating meat. The sage Sugé said:

> *All the beasts that you have slain before,*
> *Their blood is like a swamp before your feet.*
> *If that is how you go to higher realms,*
> *Then what is it that makes you sink to hell?*

And Netso has said:

> *The slaughtered sheep, the witnesses of your killing,*
> *Its blood lies in a swamp before your feet.*
> *If that is how you go to higher realms,*
> *Then what is it that makes you sink to hell?*

The sage Jawa has said:

> *The one who eats, the one whose flesh is eaten—*
> *See the difference that divides these two!*
> *The one will have his belly full for one short span;*

The other has completely lost his life!
Those who understand the fear and pain
Of those who know their final hour has come
Will rather guard the lives of other beings.

Other learned and compassionate non-Buddhist sages agree that to give protection from fear even to a single being is excellent beyond compare. It is unequaled even by the donating of mountains of gold and jewels to thousands of Brahmins, together with gifts of cows and money. Such is the opinion of certain learned and compassionate non-Buddhist sages.

If we earnestly try to do whatever is in harmony with the Buddha's message, regardless of whether it comes from ordinary people or non-Buddhist sources, treating it all as Buddha's doctrine, we will not go wrong. The *Kalachakra-tantra* says that non-Buddhist teachings that are truly excellent should also be respected. And it is said in the *Angulimala-sutra* that it should be understood that everything that is in harmony with the Buddha's teaching *is* the Buddha's teaching. All this is the teaching of Khedrup Je.

We can see therefore that meat eating is considered wrong by both Buddhists and non-Buddhists alike. One may object and ask why Gunaprabha says in his *Vinaya-sutra*, and why it is repeated in the great commentary on the same, that if the Shravakas shun meat that is pure in the three ways and can be eaten, they are behaving like Devadatta. We reply to this by pointing out that Devadatta was constantly jealous of the Buddha. He tried to injure him in many ways, throwing a boulder at him, for example, or setting an elephant on him. In addition, he created a schism in the sangha by saying to

those around him, "Look, oh-so-virtuous Gautama eats meat, but we will not eat it, for we would be harming animals otherwise." In this way, he made a rule that appeared to be more compassionate than the precept of the Buddha. In the same way, if we who are Buddha's disciples abstain from meat because we want to be honored and are envious of others, trying to appear better than they, we are indeed behaving like Devadatta. But it is quite wrong to compare with Devadatta people who abstain from meat and so on out of genuine compassion, and who do not wish to harm animals directly or indirectly. Such people are like the Buddha himself, or the Bodhisattvas, or the Buddhist practitioners like the Kadampas of old and the compassionate non-Buddhist sages and others, practitioners or ordinary people. If one makes such an error, it follows that one is implying that those who eat meat are behaving like the Buddha. And it would be logical for one to change the text of the *Vinaya-sutra* to the effect that if the Shravakas eat meat that is allowed because it is pure in the three ways, they are behaving like the Buddha. Many people will no doubt concoct such texts and exegeses—for no other reason than that they want to eat meat.

The eating of meat is perceived as something that brings the Dharma into disrepute, and thus the prohibition found in the *Lankavatara-sutra* is due to the fact that in certain countries and at certain times, even the practitioners of non-Buddhist traditions, such as the Jains, abstain from meat. This being so, the populace might well say that Buddhist monks are inferior to them, thus leading to a lack of faith in the Buddha's teaching. This is one reason the Buddha said that meat should not be eaten. In addition, since the Doctrine of the Buddha was set forth out of compassion, it stands to reason that the Buddha should have forbidden the eating of meat out of consideration for others, even if, in one's own particular case, the eating of meat were not to constitute a fault.

To be sure, if all the texts dealing with the faults of meat eating, whether in the sutras, tantras, commentaries, or biographies of teachers and their songs of realization, were gathered together, it would make for a very large book indeed.

Meat is the source of obstacles on the path. It is the seed of the lower realms and the thief of life. The consumption of meat is most certainly a cause of injury to others; no other food is the source of so much harm. Therefore everyone— masters, disciples, and benefactors—together with all compassionate and intelligent practitioners, ordinary people whether monastic or lay, powerful or weak, should from now on refrain from eating meat. We should consider it impure and as the flesh of our own parents and children. We should treat it like poison.

Let us pray to our teacher, the Buddha, visualizing him above the crown of our heads, that he might bless us to have the strength to implement this instruction; and let us visualize a stream of nectar pouring down and cleansing us.

CONCLUDING VERSE

Buddha of compassion, Refuge of us all,
Perceiving with your wisdom deep and clear
The triple time—past, present, and to come—
With loving mercy looking upon all that live as your
        dearest children,
Stay constantly above my head and bless me.

The eating of the flesh and blood of beings once our parents,
This evil food intensifies desire, which is samsara's root;
It cuts away compassion, root of Dharma.
Therefore all the faults that come from its consumption
I here again repeat in verse and tuneful song.

All you who eat this baneful food,
The flesh and blood of beings once your parents,
Will take rebirth in Screaming and the other burning hells,
There to bake and boil.

If you eat the flesh of beasts killed by another,
You will stay in such a hell for one whole kalpa's length.
But if you eat the flesh of beasts that you yourself have killed
Or commanded that another kill, for a hundred thousand
    kalpas
You will stay in hell.
And if you drink the blood of beasts slain by another,
For one whole kalpa's length not even will the names
Of the Three Jewels strike upon your ears.
But if you drink the blood of beasts that you have slain,
You will be born in hells of boiling liquid metal.
If you eat the cooked blood of a yak,
For seven lives will you attain the body of a lowly beast.
And if you eat your weight in flesh and blood,
A life, a kalpa's length, in hells of boiling metal you will
    have.
And after seven lives the selfsame destiny awaits all those
Who feast on raw red meat and gore—
And after ten for those who eat of it when cooked.

To eat the flesh of wild beasts you have killed leads down
    to hell;
And if, like beasts yourselves, you eat the creature living still,
Yama, Lord of death, will pour into your mouth
A stream of boiling molten metal.
How you will scream, consumed by inner fires!

To eat the flesh of fish that you have caught
Will lead to birth in hells that are a forest of sharp swords.
And if you eat the flesh and entrails of a dog or pig,
You will take hellish birth in filthy swamps.
All those who feast on meat and blood with strong desire
Will be reborn as spirits that consume both flesh and blood.

If, having slaughtered goats or sheep or yaks, you sell their
    meat,
You will be born an evil, deadly wraith.
To kill an animal for the sake of feasting
Leads to birth in hells of Fierce Heat.
Eating flesh and blood, you will become
A tiger, lion, wolf, or fox or cat, all frightful carnivores.
And if you feast on human flesh you will become
A male or female ghoul, or else an evil, flesh-devouring
    dakini.
And births too as an outcast will befall you:
As wicked butchers, hunters, evil ghosts.
Through having eaten meat and blood, devoid of any sense
    of shame,
In future lives you will become a madman knowing no
    restraint.

The Faults of Eating Meat

Crunching meat and bones will lead
In future lives to loss of teeth while even young.

Thus the tantras of Compassionate Avalokita
All say that meat and blood are foods that lay the three worlds
    waste.
How will you feel, with smothered mouth, with head cut off
    and heart torn out,
When others eat your flesh and drink your blood?
So use your present body as a basis of reflection—
Eat no meat, the source of harm to others.

To provide the world with meat
Unnumbered beasts are slain each day.
There is no doubt that eating meat brings harm
To other beings' lives.
No other food brings so much death.
Far worse than alcohol therefore is meat,
Which harms to such degree the lives of other beings.
This dreadful food therefore is to be shunned
By anyone who is compassionate.
The main cause of rebirth in hell is killing,
Of which the greatest pretext is the getting of flesh foods.
It's for their meat that men will slay their goats and sheep
    and yaks.
Some they smother, binding up their mouths—how terrible!

Some they catch alive and cut them open with sharp knives,
Thrusting in their hands to kill them—oh, how terrible!
Some they strike upon the flank beneath their hearts
And cut their sides apart with spear and knife—how terrible!

Some they strike upon their necks,
Cutting off their heads—how terrible!
How many different ways they have to slay their victims,
Killing creatures who were once their parents—oh, how
    terrible!
In all your lives in future may you never more consume
The flesh and blood of beings once your parents.
By the blessings of the Buddha most compassionate,
May you never more desire the taste of meat.

The Nectar
of Immortality

I bow down in devotion and take refuge in all my venerable teachers, lords and treasuries of great love that is unconditional beyond all reference. I implore them to bless me and all other beings with their great compassion, so that loving-kindness, compassion, and bodhichitta take birth in our minds.

In all the births that we have taken in the unending circles of samsara, there is no being that has not once been our mother. And when these beings nurtured us, they were as kind to us as our own mothers have been in this present life. This is something our Teacher, the Buddha, has said not once but time and time again. And who is there who could doubt his word?

This is why we must adopt the practice of the seven-point instruction in causal sequence to train our minds in bodhichitta.[1] First, we must learn to recognize that all beings have been our mothers. Second, we must be mindful of the kindness they have shown us and, third, resolve to repay them. Fourth, we must feel a tender love for them and, fifth, great compassion. Sixth, we must then cultivate the extraordinary thought of universal responsibility,[2] and, seventh, come thereby to the unsurpassable result, the attitude of bodhichitta. We must likewise train ourselves repeatedly in the practice of the equalization and exchange of self and other.[3] Then, taking our teacher and the Three Jewels as our witness, we must take the vows of bodhichitta both in aspiration and in action, and keep them.

When we have acquired an awareness of the fact that all beings have been our mothers, and when this awareness is constant, the result will be that when we see meat, we will be conscious of the fact that it is the flesh of our own mothers. And, far from putting it in our mouths and eating it, we will be unable even to take it into our hands or smell its odor. This is the message of many holy teachers of the past, who were the very personifications of compassion. What is the reason for this teaching of theirs? Goats, sheep, and so forth have all been our kind mothers at some point. Slaying them by binding their muzzles, plunging one's hands into their bodies to cut the vital artery, so that one may eat their fresh red meat—all this is nothing but the monstrous behavior of demon rakshasas. It is an action that the Buddha has denounced in many ways, saying:

> *And so in all my teachings I decry the eating of all flesh:*
> *The* Parinirvana *and* Angulimala,
> *The* Lankavatara, Hastikakshya, *and* Mahamegha *sutras.*

I do not intend here to give a detailed exposition of the wrongs entailed in the eating of meat, as these have been laid down on numerous occasions in the sutras, tantras, and shastras. Instead, I propose to give no more than a short and general explanation of the main issues.

It is said that if we eat evil food, if we consume the flesh and blood of beings who were once our mother or our father, we will, in a future life, take birth in the hell of Screaming, which, of the eighteen, is one of the hot hells. To the extent that we once consumed their flesh, so now red-hot clubs of iron will be forced into our mouths, burning our vital organs and emerging from our lower parts. We will have the experience of endless pain. And even when we are born again in this world, for five hundred lives we will take birth in monstrous and devouring forms.[4] We will become demons, ogres, and executioners. It is said too that we will be born countless times among the outcasts, as butchers, fishermen, and dyers, or as carnivorous beasts thirsting for blood: lions, tigers, leopards, bears, venomous snakes, wolves, foxes, cats, eagles, and hawks. It is clear therefore that, for the gaining of high rebirth in divine or human form, and thus for progress on the path to freedom, the eating of meat constitutes a major obstacle.

Most especially, we have been taught that the primordial wisdom of omniscience arises from bodhichitta. Bodhichitta in turn arises from the roots of compassion and is the final consummation of the skillful means of the six paramitas. It is stated in the tantra *The Perfect Enlightenment of Bhagavan Vairochana*:[5] "The primordial wisdom of omniscience arises from bodhichitta, which arises from the roots of compassion and is the fulfillment of the entire scope of skillful means." It is therefore said that one of the greatest obstacles to the birth of bodhichitta in our minds is our craving for meat. For if great compassion has not arisen in our minds, the foundation of bodhichitta is not firm. And if bodhichitta is not firm, we may well claim a hundred times that we are of the Mahayana, but the truth is that we are not; we are not Bodhisattvas of the great vehicle. From this it should be understood that the inability to eliminate the desire for meat is an impediment to the attainment of omniscience. For this reason, all those who practice the Dharma—and indeed everyone—should strive, to the best of their ability, to forsake this evil food, the flesh of their parents.

Some people will object that it is said in the teachings that one only encounters the karmic result of actions that one has actually committed; no result accrues from actions not performed. In accordance with the law of karma, therefore, if one eats the meat of animals that one has not seen to have been killed for one's consumption, if one receives no report that they have been killed for that purpose, and if one has no suspicion that they might have been so killed, no fault is incurred. "It's quite all right," they will say. "We had no hand in the killing of this sheep (or whatever other animal may be concerned). We can be sure therefore that the karma of killing will not ripen upon us; it will ripen on the killers."

This argument needs to be examined closely. Let us imagine that there is a homestead in the vicinity of a large monastery where the monks eat meat. The inhabitants of the homestead calculate that if they kill a sheep and sell its best meat in spring to the monastic community, they will make a profit on the sheep since they will keep its tripe and offal, head, legs, and hide for themselves. And the monks, knowing full well that the sheep has been slaughtered and its meat preserved, will come and buy it. The following year, the family will kill more sheep and sell the meat. And if they make a good living out of it, when the next year arrives, there will be a hundred times more animals slaughtered, and the family will get rich. Thus by trying to enrich themselves through the killing of sheep, they become butchers. They will teach this trade to their children and their grandchildren and all those close to them. And even if they do not actively teach it to others, other people will see their wicked work. They in turn will become butchers doing acts of dreadful evil, and they will set in motion a great stream of negativity that will persist until the ending of samsara. Now all this has happened for one reason only: the monastic community and others eat meat. Who therefore behaves in a more consistently evil manner than they?

If there is no meat eater, there will be no animal killer—just as in Nepal and India, there are no tea merchants because nobody drinks tea there.[6] The meat eater participates in the evil action of the animal killer. And since the meat eater's action is negative, it is quite mistaken to claim that its fully ripened effect will not be negative also. The Buddha has defined as evil any action that directly *or indirectly* brings harm to beings. And since what he says is true, it is clear that the eating of meat most certainly involves more injury to beings than the consumption of any other food. For this reason, the *Kalachakra-tantra* and its commentary both declare that, of the meat eater and the animal slayer, it is the former that has the greater sin. This being so, those who still contend that the fault of meat eaters is not so severe, or that they are not as guilty as the butcher, or indeed that they are entirely innocent, are being extremely rash. But right or wrong, why must they have such eating habits? My own belief is that they would be far better off if they could only rid themselves of their dependency.

Again, let us consider the case of a small monastery where the monks are poor and have no money, or else are thrifty and tight-fisted, or else are followers of the ancient Kadampa lineage, consuming only the three white foods. It would never even cross the minds of the lay people living nearby that they might kill animals so as to supply the monks with meat. It is said moreover that the mark of a virtuous action is that it brings direct or indirect benefit both to oneself and others. I believe therefore that if one wishes to commit oneself to an ongoing habit of goodness, there is nothing better than the resolve to abstain from meat. Those few monks who do actually have compassion should keep this in their hearts!

When a lama who eats meat goes on his summer or autumn alms tour, all his faithful benefactors think how fortunate they are that he will visit their house. "He's not just any old lama," they say. "He's an incarnate *tulku*! We must make him a good meal." Being aware of his eating habits, they slaughter a sheep and offer him the best cuts. The benefactors, for their part, make do with the entrails and think to themselves that the sheep came to a good end. How fortunate to be killed for the lama's dinner! And they tell each other it was right to put the sheep to death and that the sheep was really one of the lucky ones. But when it comes to their next life, the killers will find out how lucky *they* are!

By contrast, when the visiting lama does not eat meat, not only do the benefactors kill no animals, they hide whatever meat they have and go the whole day without it. They eat other food instead, sweet potatoes, for instance, curd and so on, so that both lama and benefactor keep themselves pure and unstained by negativity—while the sheep, for its part, stays alive and well! Let us pray that all lamas behave like this. For if they display wrong actions, other lamas and incarnations who follow after them will imitate them, and the net result will be that in summer and autumn, lamas and benefactors will join forces in planting the seeds of evil action at the very moment when they turn the wheel of Dharma! Bad for themselves and bad for others, this is the source of nothing but suffering in this life and the next. What else can one say but *lama könchok khyen,* "O Lama and the Three Jewels, think of us!"?

Then there are other people who say, "Je Tsongkhapa and his heart sons, and other learned and accomplished masters of the past, have taught, on the strength of quotations from the scriptures, that according to the vows of Pratimoksha one is allowed to eat meat that is pure in the three ways. But nowadays," they continue, "benighted Dharma practitioners, hermits and the like, talk a lot of nonsense about this and forbid the eating of meat. They are black demons, trying to deprive the monks of their food. On the contrary, it is by eating meat that the monks keep up their strength, the better to practice the Dharma. And anyway, if the sangha were not supported in this way, it would be as if their share of food were being given to butchers and ordinary people instead—which would be an extremely vicious and inconsiderate state of affairs. In any case," they conclude, "however many times people say that meat should not be eaten, the fact is that if monks and nuns are not allowed to eat meat (unstained by negativity), it follows that ordinary people should not be allowed to eat it either. And there are many good reasons for allowing Dharma practitioners to eat meat."

People who talk like this not only eat meat on their own account; they also advocate it in formal exposition and in private conversation. It is as if demons were advising them on what to eat. For all the Buddhas of the past have declared with one voice that it is on the basis of Pratimoksha that one must cultivate bodhichitta, the characteristic attitude of the Mahayana. By training in the causal vehicle of the paramitas and thence in the resultant vehicle of the Vajrayana, one must at length become the vajra holder of *all three* vows. Accordingly, we who practice the Dharma now, by following and serving our teachers, first take the vows of Pratimoksha, and then by gradual degrees we exercise our minds in bodhichitta, aiming for the practices of Mahamudra, Dzogchen, Path and Fruit, Pacification, and *Chö*. But even if we do not manage to get this far, I think that there is no one who, having taken refuge and bodhichitta, does not renew the associated vows every day.

If people take the vow early in the morning, in the presence of the Buddhas and their teacher, to cultivate bodhichitta both in aspiration and action, pledging themselves to the ways of the Bodhisattvas; and if, by the afternoon, they are harming beings—not of course directly but nevertheless indirectly—by saying that it is permissible to eat meat (consciously ignoring what the Buddha has repeatedly taught in the context of the Bodhisattva precepts—that meat, the outcome of harm done to others, should not be consumed), it can only mean that, gorged on meat, such people have lost their wits and are babbling in delirium. For this cannot be the view of a sane person. What a wonderful contrast if instead they can honestly say, "I am practicing the teachings of the sutras and the tantras, and I am sure that my conduct is unstained by faults."

Now, from the point of view of any of the three vows, when there is an important need and benefit for others and oneself, there are many special permissions that allow what is normally proscribed.[7] But it is a mistake to think that such dispensations are granted easily, without specific need. It may be objected that Khedrup Rinpoche taught, on the basis of reasoning and scripture, that it is permissible to eat meat that is pure in the threefold way. And people will no doubt refer to his book *The Outline of the Three Vows* and tell us to study it.

To be sure, we should attend to this matter with intelligence and care. There is not a single syllable of the Buddha's scriptures that the lord Khedrup has overlooked. He took them all to himself as personal instructions. He demonstrated by reasoning and scripture that the sutras and the tantras are in perfect harmony and mutually support each other, thus presenting the whole range of the Buddha's teaching as a coherent path. But when on one occasion, he said that for someone who has taken the Bodhisattva vow, the teaching of the *Lankavatara-sutra*[8] does not contradict the Pratimoksha precepts (which sanction the consumption of fish and the flesh of cloven-hoofed animals), he was merely presenting the view of those who said that to eat with desire the kind of meat prohibited in the Pratimoksha was allowed to people who had taken the Mantrayana vows. This view, however, he went on to refute.

Indeed, the eating of meat has never been permitted for those who have taken the Bodhisattva vows. On the contrary, it is clearly said that for them the consumption of meat is forbidden. This being so, those who are addicted to meat and who shift the burden of responsibility onto Lord Tsongkhapa, his heart son Khedrup, and other teachers of the past, by claiming that they allowed it, are very far from compassion, the mental soil in which the aspiration to supreme enlightenment is cultivated. They have no karmic connection with the Bodhisatttva precepts, high, medium, or low. So let them go ahead and say what they like—that they are eating meat because they are Shravakas or because they are tantrikas. And we will see what happens to them in the end!

Some people may object that, although meat eating is indeed wrong, the texts of both sutra and tantra say that if one recites the name of the Buddhas or certain mantras and *dharanis*, or if one performs a short meditation on the yidam deity together with the recitation of the mantra, the fault is purified. No wrong action is thus performed. Moreover, they say, if one does all this while concentrating on the slaughtered animal, the latter will be benefited and may even be considered fortunate, karmically speaking. Granted, they continue, when ordinary people kill goats, sheep, and yaks and eat their flesh with the blood still warm, their actions are wholly wrong. But when Dharma practitioners eat meat, and when they recite over it the words of the Buddha, charged with blessings as these are, the animal itself is greatly benefited. Therefore, they conclude, it is fine to eat meat, provided one does not have an excessive craving for it. And they also excuse themselves by saying that people and circumstances practically oblige them to eat meat.

But such people are to consider as follows—then they will understand. In the past, the compassionate Buddha said in the first turning of the wheel of Dharma that negative actions should be avoided, virtuous actions should be performed, and at all times one should have a good, kind heart.

The Buddha did not, as part of his original teachings, say that Dharma practitioners could and should eat meat. He gave no guarantee that by the recitation of his words (mantras and so on) meat eaters might be preserved from evil. It is best therefore to refrain completely from eating meat.

Why then did the Buddha speak about the possibility of purifying the evils involved in the killing of animals for meat, in the consumption of meat, and other negativities? In fact, he was referring to the negative actions accumulated in one's past lives, from beginningless samsara till the present, while one was sunk in ignorance. Even more, he was alluding to the actions performed earlier in one's present existence, when one had no other means of sustenance or was overpowered and oppressed by ignorance, craving, and aversion. But now, if one recognizes one's evil behavior for what it is; if one confesses it with a regret as powerful as if one had just swallowed deadly poison; and if one has a strong purpose of amendment, vowing never to repeat one's mistake even at the cost of one's life; if one recites the names of the Buddhas, mantras, and dharanis, and if one makes *tsa-tsas*, performs circumambulations, and so on (which, of the four strengths of confession, is the "strength of remedial practice")—one's evil actions will indeed be purified. This is the teaching.[9]

The Buddha said time and time again in the sutras such things as: "My followers should give up all evil actions that directly or indirectly injure others." One may disregard his words; one may consciously lead others to commit evil in provisioning oneself with meat. One may think, "There are always skillful means in the sutras and tantras that counteract the evil so that I shall still be pure of stain." And one can let oneself off the hook by telling oneself that there are substances to be placed into the animals' mouths and words that can be whispered in their ears and impressed upon their minds so that they will not remain in the lower realms. But to do all this reveals a complete failure to grasp the meaning of the Buddha's teaching. It is a perversion of the Dharma. To behave in this way is to act like the Chinese Muslims[10] who are outside the Dharma. For their clerics say that a great sin is committed if other people kill sentient beings but that if *they* do the killing, there is no sin. And since, they say, the slain creatures have thus encountered their religion, it will be better for them in the future. I have heard that these clerics take sheep by the neck and kill them by cutting off their heads. If this is true, there is absolutely no difference, in action and in intention, between such people and the kind of Buddhists we have just been describing. Henceforth, therefore, those who wish to eat meat should, in addition to their earlier justifications, take a few lessons from the Muslim clerics and study their tradition! They might learn a thing or two! Perhaps it will do them good and they will escape defilement!

Just look how a cat behaves. It catches a mouse and is thrilled, thinking that it is going to kill it. But then, almost as if taking pity on the mouse, the cat lets it go and plays with it—although this is certainly no game. Later, after amusing itself for a long time, it takes the mouse in its mouth, carries it off into a corner, and devours it. This is exactly what some Dharma practitioners do! They pretend to have compassion for the goat or sheep that is about to be killed, praying for it and reciting lots of *mani* mantras. Then, when the animal is killed and its flesh cooked, they take it away with them to some private place where no one can see them, and they gobble it down ravenously. Lots of people do this kind of thing.

I heard once about a cat that had caught a mouse and was carrying it off. But then the cat thought to play with it. When it let the mouse go, the mouse escaped and hid under an upturned basket lying nearby. The cat sat there looking under the basket, mewing softly, all sweetness and compassion. But when the mouse ran still deeper into its hiding place, the cat got all upset, looking up and down. Everyone around just burst out laughing! This is just how some modern Dharma practitioners behave! They put on a show of compassion and recite lots of manis as the sheep is being killed. But if the moment of death is long in coming, they get fretful and agitated. Whenever I am confronted with such a farce, I think that not only the Buddhas in the ultimate expanse must be laughing, but ordinary people in the world must be very amused too, when they hear about the antics of certain Dharma practitioners! Even so, if people *do* generate some sort of compassion and recite mantras, I do in fact think that it is of some benefit to them, even if it is not much use to the dead animal!

This whole question may be summed up by saying that, for good and compassionate practitioners of Dharma, the question as to whether one is stained or unstained by negativities is quite irrelevant. *Sincere* practitioners feel a natural, visceral compassion for the slaughtered goats and sheep as if they were their old mothers. They will have nothing to do with killing them for the sake of meat. On the contrary, they save life eagerly; they ransom animals set aside for slaughter and release them. Otherwise, it is like trying to punch someone who is not there. Showing compassion for animals after they have been killed and the meat is being eaten—reciting mantras for the animal's sake—is nothing but a silly game.

The people who do this kind of thing may appear fine and sympathetic in the eyes of the ignorant, but when you look closely, there is nothing to recommend their conduct, either in action or intent. If people twist the meaning of the Buddha's words and act evilly as we have described, this is not the fault of the Buddha's teaching. It is rather that the immaculate doctrine has been distorted by the actions and intentions of others—with the result that it becomes indistinguishable from the teachings of non-Buddhist heathens. If only we could all act in such a way that this does not happen!

Generally speaking, the Buddha's doctrine naturally makes for the welfare and happiness of beings. As it is said in the prayer, "May the Buddha's doctrine, source of every joy and benefit, remain for long!" Consequently, if human beings and animals living in the vicinity of those who say they are Buddhists coexist in happiness and peace, it is a sign that the Buddha's teachings are present. But if the reverse happens and there is harm and strife, this shows that there is no doctrine near. Nowadays, however, on the pretext of collecting for the monastic community, certain monks inflict great hardship on the villages and their inhabitants, whether human or animal.[11] It is heartbreaking to see. But here, I'd better not say too much. Anyway, nobody will listen. What is more, if I point out the personal faults of Dharma practitioners in high places, they mostly respond with angry words. And there is a danger that those who really are powerful might catch me and cut my mouth apart with a knife. So I'd better watch my step. In any case, people who are really sincere and compassionate will be helped by even the little I have said. On the other hand, no matter how much one speaks to people who are destitute of moral conscience and a sense of propriety, the result will be nothing but trouble for the speaker. In which case, as the proverb goes, "Shut your mouth is the best advice."

Our Teacher, great in compassion and skillful means, made a first rule about meat eating for the Shravakas who had taken Pratimoksha vows, specifying that the flesh of one-hoofed animals (horses, donkeys, and so forth), as distinct from the meat of cloven-hoofed animals (yaks, cows, and sheep), was not to be eaten. Later, he made another rule saying that, apart from meat that is pure in the three ways, all flesh products are proscribed. And then, in connection with the bodhichitta vow, and considering that there is not a single being who has not been our kind parent, he forbade the consumption of any kind of meat whatsoever, including the flesh of animals that have died of natural causes. It was said by the Kadampa teachers of old that the first two rules, formulated in the Pratimoksha context, were taught in the beginning for the sake of those who had an intense craving for meat. The Buddha knew that if the consumption of meat were totally prohibited from the start, such people would be unable to embrace the Buddhist teachings. Once they had entered the Dharma, however, and as their minds had been refined—and of course for the Bodhisattvas—the Buddha set forth the principle of total abstinence from meat. What the Kadampas said is very true. When the Buddha turned the wheel of the Dharma of the great vehicle, many Shravakas elevated their minds, and many of them generated bodhichitta, the supreme mind of enlightenment. They then abstained from the consumption of flesh. Consequently it is a mistake to think that all the Shravakas were meat eaters.

The great being, the second Buddha, Lord Tsongkhapa,

says repeatedly in his collected writings, and proves his words with reasoning and quotations from the scriptures, that if one understands the line of demarcation between what is permitted and what is proscribed, one will understand that the sutras and the tantras all speak with a single voice. In the context of the three vows, he explains that specific need takes precedence over prohibition. Therefore, if there is good reason for it, and in order to benefit greatly both oneself and others, it is permissible not to abstain from meat and other sense objects such as alcohol and a consort, but rather to enjoy them as an ornament of ultimate reality. But this does not mean that one is allowed to enjoy such things in the ordinary way and in the absence of perfect justification. As Lord Khedrup says in his *Outline of the Three Vows*, "All those who generate the mind of supreme enlightenment, Bodhisattvas of the great vehicle—how wonderful it would be if they abstained from every kind of meat. Even at the Pratimoksha level, except for meat that is pure in the three ways, no meat eating is permitted. Even in one's dreams one should never claim, because one craves for it, that meat eating is permissible."

These days, however, one only ever sees the meat of animals that have been slaughtered for food. It's rare indeed to come across meat that is pure in the three ways. And rarer still are the practitioners who have no desire for it. It would surely be better, therefore, if the loudmouths who go trumpeting the acceptability of meat eating were to reflect instead upon the measure of their faults!

Not only is the eating of large quantities of meat bad for one in the long term (for one's future lives); it is an obvious fact that, even in the present life, there are many who perish due to the toxins that meat may contain. Many times do we see and hear that when Dharma practitioners tell their benefactors that they need some meat, the latter go off and kill a sheep. And when the bursars in the monasteries say that they have big festivals coming, twenty or thirty sheep are bought from the nomads and are slaughtered in the autumn. This is a common occurrence in monasteries large and small. The result is that when one goes on pilgrimage to a monastery, intending to make offerings and pay one's respects, one is confronted by the spectacle of stacks of carcasses, before one has even seen the images of the enlightened beings. Now if this does not deserve to be called "wrong livelihood," then tell me what does! You "Dharma practitioners" who fail to see the direct and indirect injury done to the lives of goats and sheep, are you blind? Is there something wrong with your eyes? And if you are not blind, don't try to pretend that you don't know anything about it!

In our country, no one eats the flesh of horses, dogs, or human beings, and this is why we do not find them being killed for meat. But if there *were* a market for it, you can be quite sure that we would indeed have horse butchers, donkey butchers, dog butchers, and man butchers! Indeed, there are rumors that down in China this kind of thing actually happens. Here, in our own country, there are lots of people who eat the meat of goats, sheep, and yaks—and look at how many butchers there are! The Buddha has said, "All harm done directly or indirectly to living beings is evil. Give it up!" The very same people who understand his words go on to say that they do no harm to beings by eating meat. What demon can have possessed them? Both directly and indirectly, beings are harmed when meat is eaten. No other food is as harmful to the lives of living beings as meat!

The compassionate Buddha, skilled in means, did indeed partake of meat but only on very specific occasions, compelled by the necessity of time and place. He ate it, for example, when there was nothing else to eat and when to abstain from it would have endangered his life. He ate it also in situations where the benefactors had prepared meat that was pure in the three ways—when his refusal would have prevented the action from having its fully positive effect, and when his acceptance of it would have perfected their accumulation of merit. In other words, in circumstances of real necessity, he did partake of meat endowed with threefold purity. But if one thinks that the Buddha consumed flesh without being impelled by circumstances, and gleefully repeats this, one is in fact denigrating the Buddha and implying that he was not even a Bodhisattva. One is overlooking the passage in the *Lankavatara-sutra* where the Buddha declares, "If I am a meat eater while saying that I am not, then I am not their teacher, and they are not my disciples."

Overwhelmed by envy, Devadatta threw stones at the Buddha and set a wild elephant against him and made many other plans to kill him. He defamed the Lord, saying that he ate meat, whereas he (Devadatta) did not. In fact, Devadatta did eat meat in secret, although in front of others he rejected even the meat that was pure in the three ways. He covered up his pretense with false and hollow words, saying, "Look! The Buddha's discipline is not that of Devadatta. He's a meat eater just like anyone else!" Whoever speaks in the same sense takes the side of Devadatta. In declaring that the Buddha and his entourage were always eating pure meat at their midday meal, even when there was no need for it, such people do no honor to the Buddha and his disciples but rather shame them.

They repeat such things not only to Buddhists but to non-Buddhists too. It is thus that they defame our Teacher, implying that he was no match for Devadatta and could not refrain from eating meat. Instead of mouthing such slanders, they should keep their mouths shut. And if they cannot keep them shut, they should just fill them with excrement!

In the past, the Buddha and his disciples depended on alms for their sustenance. They did not stay in one place. They did not keep money and provisions and did not involve themselves in buying and selling. No need to say that they were completely untouched by the meat trade. Accordingly, whatever meat they consumed was of necessity pure in the threefold manner. It was quite impossible for them to be implicated in an evil kind of livelihood. But nowadays monasteries are built, and goods are stockpiled far more than for any private household. Butchers are allowed to live in the vicinity, and they in turn slaughter beasts knowing that the monks will come to buy the meat. And this is exactly what the monks do—it is simply a question of supply and demand. So it is that, thanks to buyers and killers, working hand in glove, hundreds and thousands of goats and sheep are slaughtered. Now if this entails no fault and if meat of *this* kind is pure in the three ways, it can only mean that, for such people, everything has become infinite purity![12] It means that the slaughtered beings of this decadent age are most fortunate and there is nothing wrong in harming them either directly or indirectly! It means that the Buddha has not forbidden it in his regulations, whether directly or by implication, and that to eat the flesh of animals killed by meat traders is not wrong! Not that the monks need bother about what the Buddha said, of course, for they can act with the freedom of accomplished siddhas! So let them go ahead!

Now we have a new Dharma tradition never known before! It is the Dharma of the meat-eating Buddha and meat-eating lamas, set forth for their meat-eating disciples and the butchers and purveyors who serve them! It is a tradition that advocates the extermination of the race of goats and sheep. But take care, you followers of our Teacher. If this goes on long enough, the time will come when the sheep and goats and yaks are all extinct. And then the dogs, horses, and even humans will have to watch out!

In times gone by, the gods, nagas, humans, and *gandharvas* venerated the Lord Buddha and his disciples in all sorts of ways. Many times in the sutras it is said that they offered them food prepared from "the three whites and the three sweets." It is never said that they invited them to partake of "the three reds and the three sours"! Such a thing I have never seen in any scripture. In the same way, when the second Buddha, the Lord and his heart son[13] were residing in Yerpa Lhari and elsewhere, they ate only the three whites and the three sweets, foodstuffs that the Buddha himself authorized. Nowhere in his biography or elsewhere does it say that he and his disciples ate much pure meat. Neither is it said in the life stories of Je Rinpoche (who, as an exponent of the teachings, is like the Buddha himself) and of his heart sons that they were much given to eating meat. And for his followers the purchase of pure meat is never advocated, nor is the eating of it as a satisfaction for craving.

Of course, one may object that there is the story of the householder of Rajgir who offered a meaty broth to the Buddha, which was consumed by many of the monks as well. But it should be recalled that the benefactor offered it because he knew that great merit would accrue from paying honor to the

Buddha and his followers; and he genuinely thought that broth made from meat was the best and most delicious food of ordinary folk and that therefore it was the best of offerings. For his part, the Buddha knew that if he did not accept the offering and refused to eat the soup, the action of the benefactor would fail to bear fruit and the benefactor himself would gain no merit, whereas to accept it would perfect the benefactor's accumulation of virtue. It was therefore in a complete absence of desire, as a mother might taste the flesh of her own child or as someone might apply dog's grease as a remedy for a wound, that the Buddha tasted the broth once, simply because it was good for someone else. We should not conclude from this that the Buddha made a habit of eating meat broth! In order to benefit others—no need to mention other kinds of food—the Buddha and his disciples ate even the evil, poisonous food prepared by a sorcerer!

Some may object that it was because the Shravakas, disciples of the Buddha, were always eating meat pure in the three ways that Devadatta made his rule: "The Buddha and his disciples eat meat, but we will refrain from it!" And it is true that it is said in *The Three Vows* that the Shravakas habitually ate meat pure in the three ways. But the truth is that they did so only in great need. Moreover, who can trust Devadatta and Sunakshatra and take their words as the truth? They criticized the Buddha out of jealousy. I think that all who believe, support, and repeat what they said are in fact abandoning the teaching of the Buddha and the lineage of his disciples.

It may be objected that Khedrup Je did say quite clearly, with reasoned proof and quotations from scripture, that meat pure in the threefold way should be eaten. It is quite true that if there is a real and genuine need for it, not only Khedrup Je but the Buddha himself gave his permission. When one comes across meat, one should check which is pure in the threefold way and which is not. Moreover, there are many attitudes with which meat can be eaten. Khedrup Je has never said that it is all right to eat meat out of desire. In his *Outline of the Three Vows* he says, "What does it mean to be without craving for meat? You should feel like the king and queen in the story who had to eat the flesh of their son. Examine whether that is how you feel. You should feel just like someone who is nauseated, who has no desire for food and is revolted at the sight of it, and who, if he has to eat, does so without appetite and relish." Consequently, those who claim that Khedrup Je actively advocated the eating of meat are not true disciples of Tsongkhapa and his followers. They are a disgrace to their tradition. The teaching of Je Rinpoche that, when one gains high realization, one should eat meat and drink alcohol as factors helpful to the generation of bliss and emptiness is a special instruction. It is not a general license for the ordinary consumption of meat! In any given situation, the necessity is more important than the prohibition. Therefore, we should not allow ourselves to conclude that he was advocating, without more ado and irrespective of circumstances, the eating of meat for those who simply want it!

In a situation of great necessity, it may well be that practitioners of whatever level of vows—Pratimoksha, Bodhisattva, or Mantrayana—are specially allowed, due to their capacity, to eat meat, drink alcohol, and take a consort. This is undeniable. But we who endeavor to understand the real meaning of the Buddha's teachings and those of Je Rinpoche and his spiritual sons must not be concerned exclusively with mere words. If meat, alcohol, and so forth are harmful to one's mind, they should certainly be laid aside.

Again, some may object that the teaching given in the *Kalachakra-tantra* and its great commentary ("if there is no meat eater, there will be no animal slayer") is no different from that of the Jains. It is therefore unreasonable and is not to be accepted, despite the fact that it is found in the commentary.

The Buddha has said, however, that whatever is of direct or indirect benefit to beings is permissible, even if it appears to be a negative action. Conversely, whatever brings injury to beings directly or indirectly—even if it is an ostensibly positive action—should not, on that occasion, be performed. If the accumulation of merit turns into something unwholesome, it becomes negative. Therefore, if an action accords with the Buddha's instruction—"Abandon every evil deed, practice virtue well, perfectly subdue your mind: this is Buddha's teaching"—it is to be approved, whether it is advocated by Hindu, Bonpo, Hoshang, or Muslim. "Whatever in the non-Buddhist or mundane traditions accords with the Buddha Dharma," the Buddha said, "is to be respected as my teaching." Were it otherwise, if it were forbidden to act according to the beliefs and practices of those outside the Dharma, we would have to give up all the worldly sciences. For, with the exception of the inner science of Dharma, they are practiced equally by non-Buddhists. If, therefore, the evil deed of killing does not occur, our purpose is served and this is enough.

Nevertheless, some people will still argue as follows: "There are many occasions when permission to eat meat is given to the Buddha's followers, whether in the context of the Pratimoksha, Bodhisattva, or Mantrayana vows. And even the vajra holders of the three vows eat meat that is pure in the threefold way. There is no need to single out just those who practice only according to the Pratimoksha. What is more, the Vinaya should always be adapted to the country and time in which it is observed. Meat may well be an evil food, but the kind of nourishment that is in perfect harmony with the Dharma is hard to find in Tibet. Therefore, if practitioners eat meat but at the same time train in the Buddhist teachings, not only is no fault involved, but when the practitioners gain enlightenment, they will be able to help all those who are in some way connected with them. How can the meat eating of such practitioners be compared with the behavior of ordinary people, butchers, and hunters? There may be hundreds, indeed thousands of reasons for not eating meat, but the fact is that it has to be eaten. You may well tell both practitioners and ordinary people that they should not eat meat for fear of hellfire. But no one can live without it!"

"Therefore," these people will say, "if you have a teaching whereby we can eat meat without being defiled by it, please give it to us. If you don't, then in the future you and your like should keep your advice and practice to yourselves; you should meditate on the uncertainty of the time of death and recite some manis for your own good! Your Dharma teaching is too one-sided, and you are destroying the very life of the monasteries. So shut your mouth—and if you don't stay quiet, you'll get what's coming to you! When all is said and done, isn't it precisely because you don't eat meat that you are so excitable? Isn't that the reason you're such a miserable nuisance? But no matter what we say to you, you don't listen—and away you go sounding off to the empty skies!"

Well, they are quite right. It's quite possible that no one can or will heed me. On the other hand, one or two intelligent and compassionate people might. So for their sake I feel I must set forth this teaching to the best of my ability and wits. Regarding the precepts of the three vows, again they are quite right. There are many permissions and many proscriptions. But one has to know where to draw the line. How can it be right simply to say that there is a permission to eat meat and go ahead without a moment's thought? How can we be so reckless in the way we destroy the three vows, like goats jumping into a river and injuring themselves in the process?

The situation in which eating meat is permitted is as follows. According to the Pratimoksha, one is allowed to eat meat when one is on a long journey, let us say from Kham to central Tibet, and when one can find *literally* no food other than meat—to the point where one would be risking death not to eat it. Similarly, one might be seriously ill, completely debilitated, and close to death, so that one's life depends on eating some meat. In the context of the Bodhisattva vow, it is true that if a Bodhisattva dwelling on the grounds of realization were to pass away, the light of the Doctrine would be extinguished, whereas if he or she were to live long, a great good would result for the teachings and beings. Therefore, when some great teachers grow old and need to restore their strength, they are permitted to eat meat. Again, in the context of the Secret Mantra, yogis who have gained certainty in the generation and perfection stages are allowed to partake of meat during the ganachakra and as a means of developing the realization of bliss and emptiness and so on. In brief, the eating of meat is acceptable when there is an important reason for it in terms of benefit for oneself and others.

To certain persons, special permissions may be granted that are not extended to everyone or at all times. For exam-

ple, when the monks are being exhorted to virtue, they are
admonished that they must always attend the ganachakra, that
they must not receive women in their quarters, and that they
must not drink alcohol. It is certainly true that all are bound
to behave accordingly. If, however, on account of his duties,
it is important for the steward of the monastery to stay behind, and if he gives the reason he cannot attend the ganachakra, he is granted special permission to absent himself.
Likewise, if old and sick monks ask for permission to stay in
their rooms, they are normally allowed to do so. If they have
to take some alcohol with their medicine as treatment for an
illness, they are allowed to drink it. And finally, if the monks
are dying, they are given special permission to see their mothers and sisters. Once again, the need outweighs the prohibition. The Buddha's teachings are compassionate by their
nature. Therefore, when there is a great need for something
beneficial (directly or indirectly, for others and oneself)—
something that is normally prohibited—an exception is made
and permission is granted. And this is true in the context of
any of the three vows. But if there is no such need, one cannot simply go ahead and transgress the rule. If this is clearly
understood, the Buddha's teachings, source of every good and
joy, will not be distorted, and it will be found that the sutras
and the tantras are mutually supportive. All the scriptures take
on the character of personal instructions, beneficial to one's
mind. This is crucial. If one cherishes the Buddha's teachings,
one will be a source of good to other beings; one will be able
to lead them to the certain conclusion of this and other difficult points. Since, if there is no real need for it, it is improper
for someone who has received the three vows to eat meat—
even meat that is pure in the threefold way—it is hardly

necessary to mention the consumption of the flesh of an animal that has been killed for that very purpose. If people whose wind energy is too strong need to eat meat and are unable to do without it, they should reflect on all the defects implicit in the eating of such food and work to rid themselves of all craving for it. If they do not see or hear or doubt that the animal has been killed for them by someone else, and if they buy the meat that is thus pure in the threefold way and if they eat a little of it, there is no fault.

But nowadays when lamas spend the summer and autumn traveling around the country on fund-raising missions, their sponsors and benefactors kill goats and sheep on a daily basis and offer the meat to them. The same is true for the monks when they perform ceremonies in the villages. The people slaughter lots of animals—goats, sheep, and yaks—so that they can offer the meat to the monks. Likewise, at the times of religious festivals, many animals are put to death. But if the monks and lamas eat this meat, not only are they consuming the flesh of animals that have been killed for their sake, but they are doing so in the name of the Dharma, and this is said to be much more serious than any other negative action. Such behavior should be abandoned as if it were poison!

But some people say that it is all right to eat meat and that among the lamas and teachers of today there are some who are the emanations of the Buddhas. They even say that there are butchers who are themselves emanations of the Buddhas. So what is wrong with eating meat?

Did you ever hear such laughable nonsense? The situation is like the story of the two statue makers who cheated and tricked each other so much that they were both ruined in this and future lives. Never believe such lies! Do not put your trust in such frauds and impostors, people who talk about lamas in the past who were supposed to kill animals and lead them to the higher realms, about butchers who led animals to the higher destinies or Dharma protectors who did the same. Better to believe the diamond words of the Buddha. Pay no attention to the persuasive, manipulative arguments of so-called practitioners who are ordinary people. We should look upon *all beings* as our kind parents, and in order to repay the goodness they have shown us, we must meditate daily on loving-kindness, compassion, and bodhichitta. Let us not be stained by this evil food, the flesh and blood of our very parents!

Such is my heart counsel to all who are devoted and compassionate, who have the character of Bodhisattvas. May they remember my words. May they keep them in their hearts.

This then is *The Nectar of Immortality*, an instruction that puts out the blazing fire of strong craving for the evil food that is the flesh and blood of our fathers and our mothers. It was composed by the yogi, white-footed Shabkar, who wrote it down with the good intention of benefiting the Doctrine and beings, in the pleasant solitude of the Vale of Drong, where the mind achieves its natural, limpid clarity.

Directly or indirectly, may this be of benefit to the Doctrine and beings!

May everything be auspicious—*Sarva Mangalam!*

Notes

Translators' Introduction

1. See, for example, Rapsel Tsariwa, *The Remedy for a Cold Heart* (Chamrajnagar, India: Dzogchen Shri Singha Charitable Society, 2002). This short and excellent booklet was widely distributed, free of charge, to the people who had gathered for the Kalachakra initiation in Bodh Gaya, India, in 2002.

2. *Shabkar* was a nickname meaning "white foot." He was so called because "wherever he set his foot, the country all around became white with virtue." See *The Life of Shabkar: The Autobiography of a Tibetan Yogin,* trans. Matthieu Ricard (Ithaca, N.Y.: Snow Lion Publications, 2001), xiv, 433.

3. A complete edition of Shabkar's works has recently been published simultaneously in India (New Delhi: Shechen Publications, 2003), 14 volumes in traditional *pecha* format, and in Tibet (Xining: Mtsho sngon mi rigs dpc skrun khang, 2002–3), 12 volumes in book format.

4. The autobiography of Shabkar comprises the first two volumes of the collected works. The full title of the first volume is: *Snyigs dus 'gro ba yongs kyi skyabs mgon zhabs dkar rdo rje 'chang chen po'i rnam par thar pa rgyas par 'dod rnams kyis re ba skongs ba'i yid bzhin nor bu bsam 'phel dbang gi rgyal po,* henceforth referred to as *The King of Wish-Granting Jewels.* This volume has been translated into English. See *The Life of Shabkar.* However, all citations from the autobiography in the present book are our translations.

5. See *The Life of Shabkar,* 31.

6. See *The Life of Shabkar,* 452.

7. See *The Life of Shabkar,* 460.

8. See *The Life of Shabkar,* xxx, n. 53. "Nomads of the high plateaus

of Tibet rely chiefly on meat and other animal products to subsist. They are, however, well aware of the evil involved in harming and butchering animals. It is a common practice among Tibetans to ransom the lives (*srog bslu*) of animals. Buddhists from all over the world traditionally buy fish, birds, and other animals from the marketplace and set them free. In Tibet, it is often the owners themselves who mercifully spare a certain fraction of their live-stock. In the case of sheep and yaks, they will cut the tip of one of the animal's ears and tie to the remaining part of the ear a red ribbon as a sign that the animal should never be slaughtered; the animal is then set free among the rest of the herd. The owner usually strings together all the ear-tips thus obtained and offers them to the lama, requesting him to dedicate the merit accrued through this compassionate act. Lamas and devotees often give large sums of money to herders, asking them to spare in the same way the lives of a given number of animals." Shabkar also specifies on occasion that he would offer large numbers of goats and sheep to the monasteries, but only for the purposes of providing wool and milk.

9. See Philip Kapleau, *To Cherish All Life* (Rochester, N.Y.: The Zen Center, 1986), on Buddha's last meal. The fact is that we simply do not know for certain what he ate.

10. See Kapleau, *To Cherish All Life,* for a different presentation of this point.

11. The three whites are butter, milk, and curd. The three sweets are sugar, honey, and molasses.

12. It seems likely that, as with the Hindu population nowadays, the people of ancient India were largely vegetarian. The presence of meat in a monk's begging bowl was probably a comparative rarity.

13. See *Collected Works of Shabkar,* vol. 7 (Ja), *The Emanated Scripture of Compassion (snying rje sprul pa'i glegs bam)* (New Delhi: Shechen Publications, 2003).

14. See Tulku Thondup, *Masters of Meditation and Miracles: Lives of the Great Buddhist Masters of India and Tibet* (Boston: Shambhala Publications, 1996), 203.

15. See Longchen Yeshe Dorje, *Treasury of Precious Qualities,* trans.

Padmakara Translation Group (Boston: Shambhala Publications, 2001), 185 ff.

16. See Shantideva, *The Way of the Bodhisattva,* trans. Padmakara Translation Group (Boston: Shambhala Publications, 1997), 180.

17. The mahasiddha offered spoonfuls of it to the bystanders. Those who tasted it gained accomplishment. See the lives of the eighty-four mahasiddhas and the life of Tsangnyön Heruka in E. Gene Smith, *Among Tibetan Texts: History and Literature of the Himalayan Plateau* (Boston: Wisdom Publications, 2001) 59.

18. See Dalai Lama, *The World of Tibetan Buddhism: An Overview of Its Philosophy and Practice* (Boston: Wisdom Publications, 1995), 112.

19. See Patrul Rinpoche, *The Words of My Perfect Teacher,* trans. Padmakara Translation Group (Boston: Shambhala Publications, 1998), 208.

20. See Longchen Yeshe Dorje, *Treasury of Precious Qualities,* 205–6.

21. The six ornaments are the Indian masters Nagarjuna, Aryadeva, Asanga, Vasubandhu, Dignaga, and Dharmakirti. The two supreme ones are Shakyaprabha and Gunaprabha.

22. See *The Emanated Scripture of Compassion.*

23. *bsgyur ba ldem dgongs.* See Longchen Yeshe Dorje, *Treasury of Precious Qualities,* 251.

24. See *The Emanated Scripture of Compassion.*

25. See Gyalwa Changchub and Namkhai Nyingpo, *Lady of the Lotus-Born: The Life and Enlightenment of Yeshe Tsogyal,* trans. Padmakara Translation Group (Boston: Shambhala Publications, 1999), 183, where Yeshe Tsogyal reproves the former attitude of one of her disciples.

26. See Matthieu Ricard, *The Collected Writings of Shabkar Tsogdruk Rangdrol (1781–1851)* (New Delhi: Shechen Publications, 2003), a descriptive catalog accompanying the complete works.

27. See page 120.

28. See *The Life of Shabkar,* xv.

29. In addition to the texts translated here, see also *The Emanated Scripture of Compassion* and *The Beneficial Sun (chos bshad gzhan phan nyi ma),* in *Collected Works of Shabkar,* vol. 10 (Tha) (New Delhi: Shechen Publications, 2003).

30. *rmad byung sprul pa'i glegs bam*, in *Collected Works of Shabkar,* vol. 8 (Nya) (New Delhi: Shechen Publications, 2003).

31. *The Nectar of Immortality (legs bshad bdud rtsi'i chu rgyun),* in *Collected Works of Shabkar,* vol. 12 (Na) (New Delhi: Shechen Publications, 2003)

The Faults of Eating Meat

1. *dgra bcom pa,* lit. one who destroys the enemies, that is, negative emotions.

2. The reasoning behind this idea is that semen and ova (the latter being closely associated, in the traditional mind, with the menstrual discharge) are generally thought of as unclean substances and would, taken in isolation, be an object of revulsion to most people. Just as the causes are regarded as unclean, there is no reason the result (that is, flesh) should be considered otherwise.

3. *'phags pa,* "noble being." This refers to anyone who has passed beyond samsaric existence: an Arhat, a Pratyekabuddha, a Bodhisattva abiding on the grounds of realization, or a Buddha.

4. *ma brtags pa.* All meat that is eaten carelessly without due consideration of the way it has been procured.

5. See page 60 for the resolution of the apparent contradiction of what is said earlier in the paragraph.

6. "Pure in the three ways" is a summary translation. The Tibetan terms *ma brtags, ma bslangs,* and *ma bskul* are difficult to interpret. Possibly *ma brtags* means "not earmarked," referring to animals that have been designated for slaughter; *ma bslangs* perhaps means "not taken," that is, not bought even after presentation in three successive markets; finally, *ma bskul* could mean "not ordered," in other words, not taken from animals that one has had killed for their meat.

7. These sutras all belong to the third turning of the Dharma wheel.

8. The meaning of this passage seems to be that fish was not included in the list of foods that the Buddha declared to be wholesome. Therefore if the Buddha had allowed the eating of fish, an unhealthy food, it would not make sense to describe other foods (barley, molasses, and so on) as healthy and thus advocate their

consumption. It would be as illogical as if the Buddha had advocated the inclusion of unsuitable kinds of clothing in the category of monastic garb. This appears to be the sense of the Tibetan, which, as in many places in the Kangyur, is difficult to interpret.

9. The four noble paths are those of accumulation, joining, seeing, and meditation.

10. *Saddharmasmrityupasthana-sutra.*

11. *thugs rje chen po 'khor ba dong sprug gi rgyud.*

12. *phyi mdo dgongs pa 'dus pa.* One of the root tantras belonging to the Anuyoga cycle of the Nyingma school.

13. *kun 'dus rig pa'i mdo.* A Nyingma tantra belonging to the root tantras of the Anuyoga cycle.

14. *don yod zhags pa'i cho ga zhib mo,* the detailed ritual of Amogha Pasha. This tantra focuses on the four-faced Avalokiteshvara.

15. *don yod zhags pa'i snying po.*

16. *mi g.yo ba'i rgyud.*

17. *spyan ras gzigs dbang phyug gi rtsa ba'i rgyud pad ma drva ba.*

18. *theg chen bsdus pa.*

19. With color, perhaps, derived from the bodies of insects.

20. *lta ba'i 'dod pa mdor bstan pa.*

21. *sgom rim bar ma (Bhavanakrama).*

22. *mi rtog bsgoms don.*

23. *dus khor rgyud 'grel.* Probably the first commentary on the *Kalachakra-tantra* by Chandrabhadra, the king of Shambhala and the first recipient of this teaching.

24. *rgya cher 'grel.*

25. A residual fault is a kind of fault after the commission of which only a residue of the monastic ordination remains. Before such faults are repaired, the monk or nun in question is demoted and must take the last place in the sangha, eating only the food that is left over after the communal meal.

26. Vidyadhara-pitaka constitutes, according to Gyalwa Longchenpa and other authorities, a fourth collection of teachings, namely, the tantras, which is added to the Tripitaka (the three collections of the Abhidharma, Sutra, and Vinaya).

27. Probably in the *Jatakamala.*

28. This is the mantra of Akshobya.

29. *rgyu 'bras bstan pa'i mdo.*
30. *dpe chos rin chen spung ba*, a commentary on the *dpe chos*, a Kadampa text composed by Potowa, a disciple of Dromtönpa.
31. *spon slob lo chen.*
32. *bsnyen gnas.* Pratimoksha vow consisting of nine of the ten precepts of the *shramanera* (*getsul*) ordination but taken only for a period of twenty-four hours at a time. See Longchen Yeshe Dorje, *Treasury of Precious Qualities*, 198.
33. Vimalaprabha, *dri med 'od.*
34. The fourth samaya is not to commit the root downfall of abandoning love for living beings.
35. This is an approximate translation of the following *'di la mtshungs pa zhig zhun/stu shar po gsum 'khor zhig la byas e chog mi chog na.* The meaning of the passage is uncertain.
36. That is, horses, donkeys, mules, and so on.
37. Most probably this is a reference to Jigme Lingpa, whose personal name was Khyentse Özer. Jigme Lingpa died in 1798 when Shabkar was seventeen years old. Shabkar later received the transmission of the *Longchen Nyingthig* from Lakha Drupchen, a disciple of Jigme Trinlé Özer, the first Dodrupchen Rinpoche, who was a direct disciple of Jigme Lingpa. See Tulku Thondup, *Masters of Meditation and Miracles*.
38. *Suhrllekha.*
39. The name by which Guru Padmasambhava, the Lotus-Born, is commonly known in Tibet. He was predicted by Shakyamuni Buddha as the one who would propagate the teachings of the Secret Mantra. Invited to Tibet by King Trisong Detsen in the eighth century, he succeeded in definitively establishing there the Buddhist teachings of sutra and tantra.

The Nectar of Immortality

1. The seven-point instruction in causal sequence is a practice closely associated with Atisha Dipamkara.
2. This is the decision to take responsibility for all beings and is the readiness to practice, all alone if need be, until all beings have been delivered from the round of suffering.

3. The practices of equalization and exchange are explained by Shantideva in the *Bodhicharyavatara*. See Shantideva, *The Way of the Bodhisattva*, 187.

4. *phra men pha* and *phra men ma*: monstrous creatures, both male and female, with human bodies and animal heads.

5. *bcom ldan 'das rnam par snang mdzad mngon par byang chub pa'i rgyud.*

6. This was presumably the case in Shabkar's day; in any case, the tea he was familiar with came from China.

7. *dmigs gsal gyi gnang ba brgya dgos na stong yod.*

8. "The Shravakas who eat meat are not my disciples and I am not their teacher. In decadent times to come, those possessed by demons will say that I, their teacher, have allowed the consumption of meat."

9. In other words, the teaching merely shows how the accumulated bad karma can be purified. It is not intended as a skillful means allowing one to continue to indulge in the same negativity.

10. *gya za lar.*

11. For the subsidy of religious ceremonies. See Melvyn C. Goldstein, *A History of Modern Tibet, 1913–1951: The Decline of the Lamaist State* (Berkeley: University of California Press, 1989), 34.

12. The vision of infinite purity is one of the highest realizations of the tantras.

13. Most probably Atisha and Dromtönpa.

Glossary

ANGULIMALA-SUTRA, sor phreng can gyi mdo   A Mahayana sutra belonging to the third turning of the Dharma wheel. It expounds the doctrine of the tathagatagarbha.

ARIK GESHE JAMPEL GYALTSEN ÖZER, *'jam dpal rgyal mtshan 'od zer* (1726–1803)   An important Gelug scholar of Ragya Monastery, who ordained Shabkar in 1801.

ARYA, *'phag pa*   Lit. superior, sublime, or noble one. One who has transcended samsaric existence. There are four classes of sublime beings: Arhats, Pratyekabuddhas, Bodhisattvas, and Buddhas.

ATISHA, *jo bo rje*   Also known as Dipamkarashrijnana (982–1054), abbot of the monastic university of Vikramashila, India. His visit to Tibet in 1042, at the invitation of the lama king Yeshe Ö, provided the main inspiration for the restoration of Buddhism after a period of persecution inflicted by King Langdarma. Atisha introduced the mind-training teachings, which he received from his teacher Suvarnadvipa Dharmakirti and which combine the two currents of bodhichitta teachings transmitted by Nagarjuna and Asanga. He was also a master of the tantras. His principal Tibetan disciple and successor was the upasaka Dromtön (*'brom ston*), the founder of the Kadampa school. Atisha remained in Tibet for twelve years and died there at Nyethang in 1054.

BUDDHA DIPAMKARA   A Buddha who appeared in remote antiquity. During his lifetime the ascetic Sumedha (who was reborn many kalpas later as Shakyamuni Buddha) resolved to attain enlightenment.

CHANGKYA ROLPE DORJE, *lcang skya rol pa'i rdo rje* (1717–1786)   A major scholar and prolific writer of the Gelugpa school. He had close connections with Mongolia and China, presiding over the translation of the Kangyur into Manchu and the translation and revision of the Tengyur into Mongolian. He composed the celebrated encyclopedic description of Buddhist teachings, *The Presentation of Tenets* (*grub mtha'i rnam par bzhag pa*).

CHÖGYAL NGAKYI WANGPO, *chos rgyal ngag gi dbang po* (1759–1807)   Also known as Ngawang Dargye; a Mongolian king living in the Blue Lake (Kokonor) region who was a celebrated Nyingmapa master and disciple of the first Dodrupchen Rinpoche.

DAKA, *dpa' bo*   A name given in the tantras to male Bodhisattvas; the male counterpart of a dakini. A worldly daka is a being endowed with certain preternatural powers, not necessarily beneficent.

DAKINI, *mkha' 'gro ma*   The representation in female form of wisdom. There are several levels of dakinis: fully enlightened wisdom dakinis and worldly dakinis, who possess various preternatural powers, not necessarily beneficent.

DEVADATTA, *lhas byin*   A cousin of Shakyamuni Buddha whose extreme jealousy prevented him from receiving any benefit from the Buddha's teachings.

DHARMADHATU, *chos kyi dbyings*   The expanse of ultimate reality.

DRIKUNG KYOBPA, *'bri gung skyob pa* (1143–1217)   The founder of Drikung Monastery and of the Drikung Kagyu school.

DROMTÖN, *'brom ston*   Atisha's renowned Tibetan lay disciple (1004–1064). He built the monastery of Reting (*rwa greng*), which became the center of the Kadampa tradition.

DRUKPA KUNLEG, *'brug pa kun legs* (1455–1529)   An accomplished master and poet who adopted the lifestyle of a "mad yogi," belonging to the Drukpa Kagyu school. He was famous for his songs of realization and for his eccentric, picaresque lifestyle.

GAMPOPA (1079–1153)   Also known as Dhakpo Lharje, Gampopa trained as a doctor before becoming a monk in the Kadampa tradition. He eventually met his root teacher, Milarepa, whose principal disciple he was to become and from whom he received the transmission of the Six Yogas of Naropa. Unifying the monastic and yogic paths, Gampopa exerted a decisive influence over the Kagyu tradition.

GANACHAKRA, *tshogs kyi 'khor lo*   A tantric feast offering performed within the framework of a sadhana practice.

GELUGPA, *dge lugs pa*   One of the New Translation schools, founded by Je Tsongkhapa (1357–1419). Its head is the Throne Holder of Ganden Monastery, and its most illustrious member is His Holiness the Dalai Lama.

GOTSANGPA NATSOK RANGDROL, *rgod tshang pa sna tshogs rang grol* (1608–?)   Also known as Tsele Natsok Rangdrol, he was a disciple of the famous *tertön* Jatsön Nyingpo. A highly accomplished meditator and outstanding scholar in both the teachings of the Kagyu and Nyingma schools, he received the name of Gotsangpa (dweller in the vulture's nest) because of his long retreats in the mountain caves and hermitages of the great Drukpa Kagyu master Gotsang Gonpo Dorje. His discipline was immaculate, and it is said that he never tasted a single drop of alcohol.

GUNAPRABHA, *yon tan 'od* (4th century C.E.)   A disciple of Vasubandhu and great authority on the Vinaya, he composed the celebrated *Vinaya-sutra* (*'dul ba'i mdo rtsa*).

GURU RINPOCHE   The name by which Guru Padmasambhava, the Lotus-Born, is commonly known in Tibet. He was predicted by Shakyamuni Buddha as the one who would propagate the teachings of the Secret Mantra. Invited to Tibet by King Trisong Detsen in the eighth century, he succeeded in definitively establishing there the Buddhist teachings of sutra and tantra.

GYALSE THOGME, *rgyal sras thogs med* (1295–1369)   Also known as Thogme Zangpo (*thogs med bzang po*) and Ngulchu Thogme (*dngul chu thogs med*). A great Sakya master and abbot of Bodong, celebrated by all schools for his mind-training teachings, author of *The Thirty-seven Practices of the Bodhisattvas* (*rgyal sras lag len*).

JAIN, *gcer bu pa*   Lit. naked ascetics. An important Indian religious system founded in the sixth century B.C.E. by Jina (whence Jaina or Jain), also known as Vardhamana. The Jainas or Jains advocate a very pure ethical system involving, in particular, an extreme form of *ahimsa,* or nonviolence.

JAMYANG GYAMTSO, *'jam dbyang rgya mtsho* (17??–1800)   One of Shabkar's root teachers. He was a highly accomplished master thoroughly versed in the teachings of both the Nyingma and Sarma traditions; he instructed Shabkar in the mind-training teachings and gave him many empowerments from the cycles of Nyingma treasures, including the *Longchen Nyingthig* of the vidyadhara Jigme Lingpa.

JIGME LINGPA (1730–1798)   One of the most important figures in the Nyingma lineage, an incarnation of both the master Vimalamitra and the Dharma king Trisong Detsen. He was closely associated with Gyalwa Longchenpa, whom he encountered in a series of important visions. His Dharma treasure, the *Longchen Nyingthig,* remains to this day one of the most important and widely practiced meditative systems in the Nyingma school.

JNANASHRIBHADRA, *ye shes dpal bzang po*   An Indian master and author of a commentary on the *Lankavatara-sutra,* the *Arya-lankavatara-vritti,* preserved in the Tengyur collection.

JNANAVAJRA, *ye shes rdo rje*   An Indian master and author of a commentary on the *Lankavatara-sutra*, the *Tathagata-hridayalamkara* (*de bzhin gshegs pa'i snying po rgyan*), preserved in the Tengyur collection.

KADAMPA, *bka' gdams pa*   Inspired by Atisha and founded by his disciple Dromtön, this school placed great emphasis on the mind-training teaching of bodhichitta and pure observance of ethical discipline. It exerted a decisive influence on the entire Tibetan tradition.

KAGYUPA, *bka' brgyud pa*   One of the New Translation schools of Tibetan Buddhism, founded by Marpa the Translator (1012–1099). This school subsequently divided into many subschools, the most well known nowadays being the Karma (or Dhakpo) Kagyu, Drikung Kagyu, Drukpa Kagyu, and Shangpa Kagyu.

KALACHAKRA-TANTRA, dus 'khor gyi rgyud   A tantra taught by the historical Buddha Shakyamuni to Chandrabhadra (*zla ba bzang po*), king of Shambhala, who was an emanation of the Bodhisattva Vajrapani. It belongs to the nondual class of Anuttara tantras and presents a complete path to enlightenment, together with an elaborate system of cosmology.

KAMALASHILA (713–763)   The principal disciple of Shantarakshita and an exponent with him of the Yogachara-Madhyamika school. He was invited to Tibet, where he successfully debated against the Chinese master Hoshang Mahayana, thereby establishing the gradual approach of the Indian tradition as normative for Tibetan Buddhism.

KANGYUR, *bka' 'gyur*   The canonical collection of sutras and tantras translated into Tibetan.

KATYAYANA   A disciple of Buddha Shakyamuni. He attained arhatship and committed to writing a part of the Abhidharma teachings.

KHEDRUP JE, *mkhas grub rje dge legs dpal bzang* (1385–1438)   One of the two most important disciples (the other being Gyaltsap Je) of Je Tsongkhapa, founder of the Gelugpa school.

KRISHNAPA, *slob dpon nag po* (11th century)   An Indian master and teacher of Atisha.

LANKAVATARA-SUTRA, lang kar gshegs pa'i mdo   A Mahayana sutra of the third turning of the Dharma wheel that belongs, according to Gyalwa Longchenpa, Karma Rangjung Dorje, and Kongtrul Lodrothaye and others, to the teachings of the ultimate meaning. Chandrakirti classified this sutra as being of expedient meaning, in line with the teaching of the *Aksayamatinirdesha-sutra*, which, however, does not mention or take into account the three turnings of the Dharma wheel. For an excellent discussion of this topic, see Susan K. Hookham, *The Buddha Within: Tathagatagarbha Doctrine According to the Shentong Interpretation of the Ratnagotravibhaga* (Albany: State University of New York Press, 1991).

LONGCHENPA, *klong chen rab 'byams*   Regarded as the greatest genius of the Nyingma tradition, an incomparable master and author of over 250 treatises.

MAHAPARINIRVANA-SUTRA, mya ngan las 'das pa chen po'i mdo   A Mahayana sutra of the ultimate meaning belonging to the third turning of the Dharma wheel and expounding the doctrine of the tathagatagarbha.

MATERIALISTS or CHARVAKAS, *rgyang 'phen pa*   Name of the ancient Indian philosophical school professing materialistic nihilism. The Charvakas denied the law of karma and the existence of past and future lives.

MILAREPA, *mi la ras pa* (1040–1123)   One of the greatest yogis and poets of Tibet. He was one of the foremost disciples of Marpa the Translator, founder of the Kagyu lineage.

NAGARJUNA, *klu grub*   A great second-century master of the Mahayana and founder of the Madhyamika system of thought closely associated with the *Prajnaparamita-sutras*.

NYAKLA PEMA DUDUL, *nyag bla pad ma bdud 'dul* (1816–1872)   A celebrated master from Nyarong in the east of Tibet, who accomplished the rainbow body.

NYINGMAPA or Ancient Translation School, *rnying ma*   The original tradition of Tibetan Buddhism. Its adherents study and practice the tantras, and their related teachings, translated in the first period between the introduction of the Buddha Dharma to Tibet in the eighth century and the period of the new translations inaugurated by Rinchen Zangpo (958–1051) after the persecution by Langdarma.

PATRUL RINPOCHE, *dpal sprul o rgyan 'jigs med chos kyi dbang po* (1808–1887)   A highly accomplished master of the Nyingma tradition, from eastern Tibet; the author of numerous works, of which *The Words of My Perfect Teacher* (*kun bzang bla ma'i zhal lung*) is one of the most celebrated. He was famous for his nonsectarian approach and renowned for his compassion and the extraordinary simplicity of his lifestyle.

PHAGMO DRUPA, *phag mo gru pa rdo rje rgyal po* (1110–1170)   A disciple of Gampopa and founder of the Phagdru tradition of the Kagyu school. Many of his disciples attained high realization.

PRATIMOKSHA, *so sor thar pa*   Lit. individual liberation. This term is used to refer to the eight kinds of Buddhist ordination (both monastic and lay), together with their connected vows and disciplines (including the temporary vow of upavasa, or twenty-four-hour discipline).

PRATYEKABUDDHA, *rang sangs rgyas*   A "solitary Buddha," one who, without relying on a teacher, attains the cessation of suffering by meditating on the twelve links of dependent arising.

Pratyekabuddhas realize the no-self of the person and go halfway to realizing the no-self of phenomena. In other words, they realize the no-self of perceived phenomena but not that of the perceiving mind.

RAKSHASA, *srin po*   A class of dangerous, flesh-devouring nonhuman beings figuring in Hindu and Buddhist mythology.

RETING TRICHEN, *rwa greng khri chen blo bzang ye shes bstan pa rab rgyas* (1759–1816)   The second throne holder and abbot of the monastery of Reting, founded by Atisha's great disciple Dromtönpa.

SAKYAPA, *sa skya pa*   One of the new translation schools of Tibetan Buddhism founded by Khön Könchog Gyalpo and associated with the great monastery of Sakya. The Sakya lamas were, for a time, the rulers of Tibet.

SARMA, *gsar ma*   The new translation schools of Tibetan Buddhism (namely, Kagyupa, Sakyapa, and Gelugpa) founded in the period following the persecution by Langdarma.

SHIKSASAMUCCAYA, bslabs pa kun las btus pa   An anthology of texts taken from important Mahayana sutras, compiled by Shantideva.

SHRAVAKA, *nyan thos*   One who hears the teachings of the Buddha, practices them, and transmits them to others with a view to his or her personal liberation from samsara. Shravakas are practitioners of the Root Vehicle, or Hinayana, which is often for that reason called the Shravakayana.

TAKLUNG THANGPA, *stag lung thang pa bkra shis dpal*   Taklung Thangpa (1142–1210), a disciple of Phagmo Drupa and founder of the Taklung Kagyu school. He was known for his realization of Mahamudra attained through devotion.

TARANATHA KUNGA NYINGPO (1575–1635)   A famous scholar and the most eminent master of the Jonang tradition. One of the leading exponents of the "extraneous emptiness" view (*gzhan stong*).

TATHAGATA, *de bzhin gshegs pa*   Lit. thus gone, an epithet of Buddha or buddhahood.

TATHAGATAGARBHA, *de bzhin gshegs pa'i snying po*   The essence of buddhahood, the luminous and empty nature of the mind, which is present, albeit veiled, in all sentient beings. When the obscuring veils are removed and it is revealed, it is Tathagata, or buddhahood.

TENGYUR, *bstan 'gyur*   The canonical collection of Indian commentaries on the Buddhist scriptures translated into Tibetan.

TSONGKHAPA, *tsong kha pa*   Otherwise known as Lozang Drakpa and Je Rinpoche, the founder of the Gelugpa school. He founded the monastery of Ganden in 1410. A great scholar, revered as a manifestation of Manjushri.

UPAVASA, *bsnyen gnas*   The twenty-four-hour Pratimoksha vow, consisting of nine precepts and taken by lay people.

VIDYA MANTRA, *rig sngags*   Mantras are generally said to be of three kinds: vidya mantras, dharani mantras, and secret mantras. These categories refer respectively to the skillful means of compassion, the wisdom of emptiness, and their nondual union.

VIMALAMITRA, *dri med bshes gnyen*   One of the greatest masters and scholars of Indian Buddhism. He went to Tibet in the ninth century where he taught and translated numerous Sanskrit texts. He was one of the principal sources, together with Guru Padmasambhava, of the Dzogchen teachings of Tibet.

VIMALAPRABHA, dus 'khor 'grel chen dri med 'od   A very extensive commentary on the *Kalachakra-tantra*, and the basic textual source for the entire Kalachakra system. It was composed by Kalki Pundarika, one of the Dharma kings of Shambhala, and still exists in Sanskrit.

VINAYA, *'dul ba*   The corpus of the teachings on ethical discipline given by the Buddha.

VINAYA-SUTRA, 'dul ba'i mdo rtsa   A commentary on the Vinaya teachings, composed by Gunaprabha.

YESHE Ö, *lha bla ma ye shes 'od*   King of Tibet and member of the Chögyal dynasty. He assumed the kingship in Ngari, western Tibet, with the name of Tsenpo Khore. Later he abdicated in order to become a monk and was subsequently known as Lha Lama Yeshe Ö. In a bid to revive Buddhism in his country, he sent a party of twenty-one young men to Kashmir to learn Sanskrit and to study the teachings. It was in response to his generous offerings that Atisha accepted his invitation to visit Tibet.

Bibliography

Changchub, Gyalwa, and Namkhai Nyingpo. *Lady of the Lotus-Born: The Life and Enlightenment of Yeshe Tsogyal.* Translated by the Padmakara Translation Group. Boston: Shambhala Publications, 1999.

Dalai Lama. *The World of Tibetan Buddhism: An Overview of Its Philosophy and Practice.* Boston: Wisdom Publications, 1995.

Goldstein, Melvyn C. *A History of Modern Tibet: The Decline of the Lamaist State.* Berkeley: University of California Press, 1989.

Kapleau, Philip. *To Cherish All Life.* Rochester, N.Y.: The Zen Center, 1986.

Longchen Yeshe Dorje, Kangyur Rinpoche. *Treasury of Precious Qualities.* Translated by the Padmakara Translation Group. Boston: Shambhala Publications, 2001.

Page, Tony. *Buddhism and Animals.* London: UKAVIS Publications, 1999.

Patrul Rinpoche. *The Words of My Perfect Teacher.* Translated by the Padmakara Translation Group. Boston: Shambhala Publications, 1998.

Ricard, Matthieu. *The Collected Writings of Shabkar Tsogdruk Rangdrol (1781–1851).* New Delhi: Shechen Publications, 2003.

Shabkar, Tsogdruk Rangdrol. *The Collected Works of Shabkar Tsogdruk Rangdrol.* Vol. 1 (Ka), *The King of Wish-Granting Jewels, the Autobiography of Shabkar Tsogdruk Rangdrol (snyigs dus 'gro ba yongs kyi skyabs mgon zhabs dkar rdo rje 'chang chen po'i rnam par thar pa rgyas par bshad pa skal bzang gdul bya thar 'dod rnams kyi re ba skongs ba'i yid bzhin gyi nor bu bsam 'phel dbang gi rgyal po).* New Delhi: Shechen Publications, 2003.

———. *The Collected Works of Shabkar Tsogdruk Rangdrol.* Vol. 7 (Ja),

The Emanated Scripture of Compassion (snying rje sprul pa'i glegs bam). New Delhi: Shechen Publications, 2003.

—————. *The Collected Works of Shabkar Tsogdruk Rangdrol*. Vol. 8 (Nya), *The Wondrous Emanated Scripture (rmad byung sprul pa'i glegs bam)*. New Delhi: Shechen Publications, 2003.

—————. *The Collected Works of Shabkar Tsogdruk Rangdrol*. Vol. 9 (Ta), *The Emanated Scripture of Pure Vision (dag snang sprul pa'i glegs bam)*. New Delhi: Shechen Publications, 2003.

—————. *The Collected Works of Shabkar Tsogdruk Rangdrol*. Vol. 10 (Tha), *The Beneficial Sun (chos bshad gzhan phan nyi ma)*. New Delhi: Shechen Publications, 2003.

—————. *The Collected Works of Shabkar Tsogdruk Rangdrol*. Vol. 12 (Na), *The Nectar of Immortality (legs bshad bdud rtsi'i chu rgyun)*. New Delhi: Shechen Publications, 2003.

—————. *The Life of Shabkar: The Autobiography of a Tibetan Yogin*. Translated by Matthieu Ricard. Ithaca, N.Y.: Snow Lion Publications, 2001.

Shantideva. *The Way of the Bodhisattva*. Translated by the Padmakara Translation Group. Boston: Shambhala Publications, 1997.

Singer, Peter. *Animal Liberation*. New York: Ecco Press, 2001.

Smith, E. Gene. *Among Tibetan Texts: History and Literature of the Himalayan Plateau*. Boston: Wisdom Publications, 2001.

Thondup, Tulku. *Masters of Meditation and Miracles: Lives of the Great Buddhist Masters of India and Tibet*. Boston: Shambhala Publications, 1996.

Tsariwa, Rapsel. *The Remedy for a Cold Heart*. Chamrajnagar, India: Dzogchen Shri Singha Charitable Society, 2002.

Printed in the United States
by Baker & Taylor Publisher Services